EASY-TO-MAKE
GIFTS
FOR THE
BABY

CINDY HIGGINS

WILLIAMSON PUBLISHING
CHARLOTTE, VERMONT 05445

Library of Congress Cataloging-in-Publication Data

Higgins, Cindy.
  Easy-to-make gifts for the baby.

Includes index.
  1. Handicraft.   2. Infants' supplies.   3. Sewing
I. Title.
  TT157.H455   1988   745.5   87-37176
  ISBN 0-913589-34-9

Cover and interior design: Trezzo-Braren Studio

Printing: Capital City Press

Williamson Publishing Co.
Charlotte, Vermont 05445

Manufactured in the United States of America

First Printing: March 1988

CONTENTS

To
Babies, good neighbors, soda pop,
Aunt Nancy Gale and Kirby, Sally Ruth,
and to my all-time best Dave, the
Montgomery's finest production.

♥

INTRODUCTION

Babies are special.

There's no question about it.

And making personalized presents for newborns and growing tots is special and fun, too! When it comes to baby gifts, homemade is definitely best. Somehow storebought (no matter how expensive) never quite measures up to a handmade, home-crafted gift from the heart.

Each project in this book is designed to be as attractive, inexpensive, and simple as possible. Most projects can be crafted in less than an hour and yet they are so practical and attractive, they'll be cherished for years to come.

Beginners and those who think they are "all thumbs" should be able to make every item in this book. Experienced crafts people, too, will appreciate the diversity of projects and might want to incorporate the options that are included with most projects, or further refine some projects depending on special areas of expertise and interests. Basically, these projects are starting points — you can expand on ideas using your imagination and creativity.

Many of these gifts — the quilt, the blanket, the doll bed and bedding, the rocking chair, to name a few — are the kinds of gifts families cherish and keep for generations. No, they are not the time-consuming fancy finished projects of years ago or like you might dream of having time to make — but they are very attractive, show-stopper gifts, and people love receiving and using them. They are fun to make and a delight to give.

Give holidays and special occasions an extra sparkle by treating the people in your life to these thoughtful presents created by you. They make excellent Christmas stocking stuffers, great birthday gifts, are special keepsakes at Easter or Valentine's Day, or just to say "you're special."

Some gifts in here, such as the washmittens, bibs, and soft toys, are wonderful for baby showers. Make several of these easier, smaller projects, wrap each individually, and fill a basket with your creations for an unforgettable shower present. What fun for the lucky recipients to open and use!

Many of the crafts included are especially appropriate for teens and preteens to make for siblings, neighbors, and the children they babysit for. The crafts are such that the teens will derive plenty of satisfaction from a job well done, and, needless to say, the recipients will be thrilled with a lovely gift from someone they care about.

Safety First – Always

The projects in this book are geared for newborn infants up to 3 year-old toddlers. Many are clearly for newborns to eighteen months old. Some, such as wall sculptures or stuffed monkeys or dolls are always appropriate, as long as removable parts are modified for infants and toddlers still putting things in their mouths.

Caution: Toys with buttons, pompons, moveable eyes, sequins, rhinestones, and other adornments are not appropriate for infants and some toddlers. Do not put in cribs, playpens or carriages. If you wish to make these items for younger children, embroider designs and faces on them for the same effect, or top-stitch and use appliques and sewn-on bric-a-brac for decoration.

Even for older toddlers, sew button eyes and other notions on extra firmly and check (and reinforce) frequently. If you notice a child sucking or pulling on button-type eyes of any toy, gently take the toy away or remove buttons from the toy immediately. My own preference is to not put this type of toy around children who still put things in their mouths.

All wooden toys in this book are sanded and sealed for safety. Be sure not to leave sharp edges or rough, splintering surfaces. Please don't take any sanding shortcuts.

Before you begin, read the section on materials, design hints, and construction methods. If you still have questions after reading this section, ask sales personnel at the stores that stock the materials you will be using for further information.

Most of all enjoy making and giving these home-crafted gifts. Set aside some quiet time to work on your crafts (perhaps with a cup of tea by your side). Other times, invite your older children and teenagers to join you in preparing a gift together. Craft-time, especially with *Easy-to-Make Gifts for the Baby* is a special time indeed. ❤

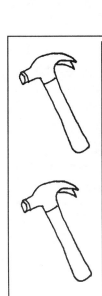

· 1 ·

Easy-to-Make How To

Project
Construction
Overview

The finished look your project will have depends on you. You can follow or alter the instructions to suit your fancy, skills, and needs. Two people can follow the same directions, and the results will be strikingly different. The key to each project is your imagination, your personal preferences, and your willingness to experiment.

As Heywood Broun, a sportswriter from yesteryear, said: "There are one hundred and fifty-two distinctly different ways of holding a baby — and all are right." That advice goes for your creations, too. Follow your aesthetic instincts, keep in mind a child's safety, and you should be pleased with the results.

Try new ideas or savor the old. If you thought teddy bears, butterflies, and lambs were the only nursery-appropriate animals, you're in for a surprise! Piglets, monkeys, pandas, sheep, ladybugs, dinosaurs, and even flamingos look great, too.

Personalize objects not only with a child's name or birthdate, but also with designs of a parent's hobby (tennis racquet, camera) or an older toddler's interests (swing, drums, favorite book).

Color choice will play a crucial role in your finished work. Primary colors are thought to attract an infant's eyes better than muted shades while pastel colors have a softness that many children and adults find more attractive. Or maybe you prefer neutral and earth tone colors. It's up to you to choose!

Materials, too, are an important choice, especially in fabrics. Soft, slick, furry, smooth, rough — the range in choices is amazing. The collection of nursery prints and pre-quilted fabrics is growing steadily. A general rule for choosing a fabric print is to match the size of the object with the print size. Because many of the projects in here are small-sized, you'll find that smaller prints, such as gingham checks, work well, but that's not to say larger, bolder prints can't be incorporated into your creations.

Whatever you decide, just remember that a homemade gift is always welcome and rewarding to make. And wonderful to receive!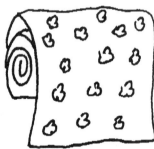

SIZING DESIGNS

The easiest way to enlarge or reduce designs is to use a photocopying machine. Many machines have pre-set reduction and enlargement percentages, such as 65%, 95%, or 120%, but others can be set for any percentage.

Or you can use the *grid method* for sizing. A grid is made by ruling horizontal and vertical lines, creating equal-sized squares over the design you are enlarging. Each square represents a certain inch size. If a design is drawn on a grid where one square equals one inch, and you want to double the design size, make 2-inch squares, and transfer the design square by square. Make your own grids with a ruler

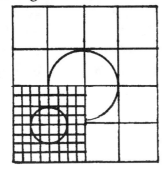

and pencil, and adjust design sizes to fit your needs.

There are other ways to size designs, but these two methods are the easiest for exact design sizing. You can always draw designs free-hand yourself.

TRANSFERRING DESIGNS AND PATTERNS TO MATERIAL

Use tailor's chalk or an erasable pen to draw directly on fabric. *For copying patterns in this book,* lay a piece of light-weight white paper, such as typing paper, on the pattern; trace and cut. Pin the pattern to the fabric, or cut or trace around patterns on wood projects. Other pattern transfer aids are carbon paper (for wood projects that are going to be painted), dressmaker's carbon and tracing wheel, or "disappearing" tracing paper (which is constructed so that marks will disappear in 72 hours or be wiped off instantly with a damp cloth). For embroidery projects, you can also sew through

washable transfer paper onto the project; the paper will dissolve when sprayed with water or washed.

DRAWING HINTS

To make symmetrical designs and patterns, fold a piece of paper in half and draw half of the shape; cut and open out. Or draw one side of the shape with a dark marker on light-weight, white paper; fold the paper in half so the drawing is visible underneath the finished side. Trace the drawing outline and cut. If the drawing is too faint for tracing, put the paper on a window during the day for greater visibility.

Drawing tools, such as a t-square, ruler, 45-or-30 degree angle triangles, will help in ruling straight lines. Place the triangle on the t-square for making angled lines.

Circles can be made by tracing around a dish or other circular item, or by using a compass. Put a small piece of heavy paper under the compass point so the project surface isn't marred. For making larger circles, make a simple but effective compass with a piece of string tied to a pencil. Hold the string end at the circle center, determine the radius, and draw the circle outline with a pencil. Or draw a cross and connect cross ends with curved lines.

Use a flexible plastic ruler or flexible plastic curve to make curved lines. Hold ruler ends at start and finish of projected curved line. Trace curve along the inside of bent ruler.

Templates or stencils, both of which have cut-out shapes, can be used to draw designs that are repeated.

SEWING STITCHES

A sewing machine is not necessary for the projects in this book.

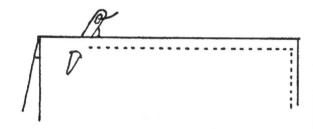

Topstitch
Use the running stitch on the right side of fabric to join all fabric layers. The topstitch is often used to add detail and soft-sculptured effect.

Whipstitch
Insert needle into fabric, bring needle and thread over fabric edge, and insert needle 1/4" to the right of starting point to begin the next stitch.

Slipstitch
Pick up a few strands of fabric on turned-under edge, go 1/4" to the right on other turned-under edge to pick up thread strands again, and continue. Stitches should not show on the fabric outside. Use to close up openings on seamed projects.

Running Stitch
Slip needle in and out of fabric piece or lined-up pieces. Use for hand-sewn seams and attaching appliques.

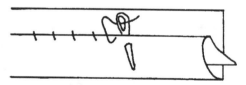

Hemming Stitch
Pick up a few threads of fabric with needle, insert needle into turned-under edge of hem, draw needle out, and repeat steps.

Gathering Stitch
Baste (use long running stitches) beneath fabric edge. When basting is finished, gently pull thread at one end to gather fabric.

EMBROIDERY STITCHES

Straight Stitch
Insert needle into fabric, draw thread through, and bring needle out where next stitch begins.

Cross-Stitch
Make a row of slanted stitches. Work over slanted stitches with stitches slanted in opposite direction.

Back Stitch
Insert needle, bring out a stitch ahead, and insert needle a stitch behind.

Blanket Stitch
Make an upright stitch to the right with needle pointed down. Keep thread under needle and catch thread loop with needle.

Chain Stitch
Insert needle where thread was brought out. Keep thread under needle to form small loop. Draw needle through loop for next insertion.

Satin Stitch
Use straight stitches closely sewn together to fill in design areas.

MATERIALS

ADHESIVES

Adhesive comes in many forms. Read the package instructions before using. Here are some you may be using for project construction:

Glue sticks are used in electric glue guns. This glue is good for exact placement and quick coverage of large areas. It bonds in sixty seconds.

Rubber cement is applied with a brush and is best for temporary bonding. Excess dry glue can be rubbed off with fingers.

Spray adhesive can be used on most surfaces, except wood. Depending on how the spray is used, it can be temporary or permanent.

White glue dries clear and comes in bottles, sticks, and balled-tipped tubes. Use to bond cloth, paper, polystyrene foam, and pottery.It is not recommended for metal, photographs, and things that will get wet or be heated. *Fabric glue*, a type of white glue, may dissolve when washed.

Wood glue or *carpenter's glue* is for hard and soft woods. Use only on unfinished wood. A clamp, such as a C-clamp will help wood parts bond while drying.

CUTTING TOOLS

Cutting tools needed for these projects include scissors, a craft knife, and saws.

A *craft knife,* such as the X-acto brand, is used for cutting stencils, paper, cardboard, and balsa wood. A #10 blade is best for paper and stencils. Change the blade frequently to avoid producing jagged edges.

A *saber saw* (or *jigsaw*) is an inexpensive electric saw that will make any of the wood projects in this book. This saw rips, crosscuts, and makes curves on wood thicknesses under 2 inches. Three non-electric saws that together will do the work of a saber saw are a *hand-saw* with a 7" blade for straight cuts and a *coping saw* or *compass saw* for curves and intricate shapes.

SEALANTS

Sealants protect your projects from wear and dirt. They can be applied with an aerosol can or brush and have either a satin or gloss finish. Some wood sealants have a built-in wood stain.

Polyurethane is an excellent sealant for wood projects. It is resistant to alcohol, household chemicals, weathering, and is lead-free, and, therefore, safe for children.

Aerosol acrylic sprays can be used to seal wood, ceramic, and other materials.

Fabric protector sealants should be used on (non-washable) fabric projects to help them stay clean.

FABRICS

Fabric for these projects will generally be cotton, felt, or fake fur.

Cotton is bought by the yard and is typically 45" wide. There are many small country prints and baby prints available which enhance these projects.

Fake fur (known as fun fur, pile, or robe fur) should be cut and seamed with fur edges pushed away from tools while working. You can buy an old fur coat at a rummage sale or second-hand store and use this for fur projects, too.

Felt, bought by the yard or the piece, is an excellent craft fabric because it does not ravel, making it good for applique work. It can be either sewed or glued and should not be washed. Often you can buy remnant felt pieces in order to collect various colors. Save tiny scraps, too, because that is all you need for a clown's cheeks or a wagging puppy tongue.

Pre-quilted fabric has batting attached to the wrong side, is top-stitched, and may be less than 45" wide. *Quilted fabric* can be made by basting batting to wrong side of fabric, marking evenly spaced lines on fabric right side, and top-stitching along lines through both layers.

WOOD

Wood may be bought at hardware stores or lumber yards. Store personnel will, if requested, cut wood for you. Most of the wood projects in this book can be made from scraps of wood that you might get from friends or other sources. Wood comes in different quality grades. Select pieces that have few knots or blemishes.

Plywood comes in exterior or interior grades in 4' by 8' and 2' by 4' sheets. Make sure to use interior grade plywood, which generally has a smoother surface than exterior. Take care to avoid wood splintering when sawing or placing screws in plywood. Splintered or lifted-up wood can be glued back in place.

SEWING AIDS

Batting, used for padding, is sold by the yard (48" or 96" width) or in bagged rolls (such as 45" x 36", 45" x 60", 81" x 96"). *Quilt batting* is thicker than *single-thickness batting* and is good to use when projects require extra thickness.

Stuffing for all projects is *polyester fiberfill,* which is generally sold in bags. This type of stuffing is light-weight, washable, flame-resistant, and does not clump or bunch up as cotton stuffing can.

Self-gripping fastener, commonly sold under the brand name Velcro, comes in different widths and is sold by the inch or packaged pre-cut lengths.

Fabric fusing aids such as fusible tape, web, or glue, join fabric pieces without sewing. These bonds are retained when washed. There are also "basting" tapes and thread that will hold fabric, but dissolve after being washed.

Embroidery floss comes in six-strand skeins. Use three strands together when embroidering.

Thread used in projects is polyester-cotton sewing thread.

GENERAL CRAFT AIDS

Stencils can be bought pre-cut, or you can cut your own with a craft knife from a hard plastic sheet. Cut sheet on a piece of glass to avoid dulling knife blade. *To transfer color* into the stencil areas, put stencil paint or stencil crayon rubbings on a plastic scrap, and load stencil brush with pigment. Brush with a circular movement, making sure the outline area is throughly brushed with color. Clean brush with mineral spirits.

Paint is either water- or oil-based. Enamel water-based paint is recommended for all projects in this book, especially because brush clean-up is so easy.

Sandpaper comes in five different grades. The sandpaper you might use for these projects is *Very Fine,* when sanding between layers of sealing or paint; *Fine,* for the final sanding before painting or sealing; and *Medium,* for rough edges and removing stains.

USEFUL DESIGNS AND DECORATIONS

Here are some designs you may want to incorporate into your hand-crafted projects. You can also get design ideas from cartoon figures, storybook characters, children's television shows, and even from patterns on children's clothing.

These designs can be enlarged in transfer or transferred as sized. You can also develop templates and stencils from any of these designs, as many of them work effectively in repetition.

2

In My Room

* book * shelf *

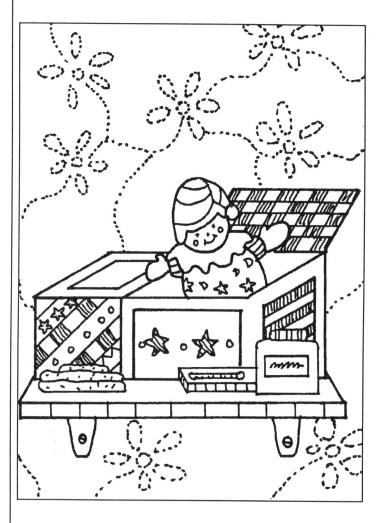

MATERIALS

$\frac{1}{2}$" interior plywood (15" x 12$\frac{1}{2}$")

1" brads or finishing nails (3)

carbon paper

pencil

sandpaper

paint

polyurethane sealant

shelf brackets – 4" x 5" (2)

Paint Shelf in bright primary colors!

1   Cut one 7 1/2" x 15 1/2" shelf backing and one 5 1/2" x 14" shelf base.

2   Enlarge shelf design below by 50%. Trace design to shelf backing using carbon paper.

3   Cut backing top edges to match design outline. Sand edges.

4   Plot design colors. Paint design on backing. Paint base, sides, and back a solid color.

5   Nail backing on top of base. Seal. Screw shelf brackets on for hanging.

* rocking * chair *

MATERIALS

¾" interior plywood (2' x 4')

marking device

ruler

saw

wood glue

#4 1½" wood screws (12)

sandpaper

paint

polyurethane sealant

* * * * * * *

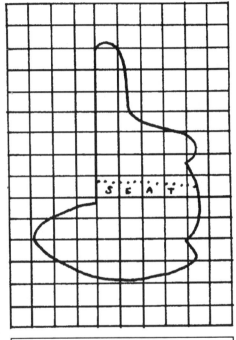

one square = 2"

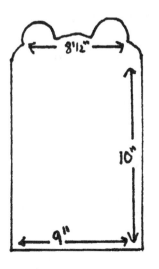

1 Draw and cut chair back and two sides from wood using diagram. (Ears on chair back are 3"-diameter semicircles.)

2 Cut a 10" square for seat and two 10"x 1" seat braces.

3 Glue and screw all pieces together. The back is placed between sides, seat joins back (represented on dotted line of diagram), seat front ends are flush with sides, and braces are below seat.

4 Sand when glue is dry.

5 Paint chair, bow, and facial features; then seal.

Delete bow, and glue fake fur to chair insides.

nursery✳organizer

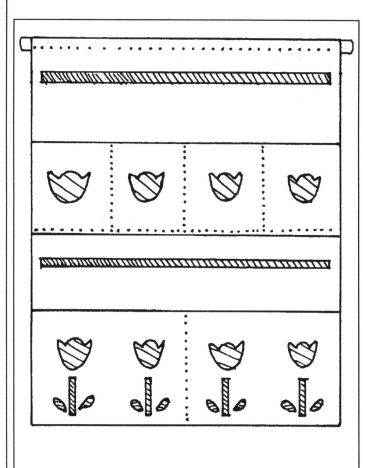

MATERIALS

white cotton canvas – 54" width ($^1/_2$ yd.)

scissors

thread

iron

chalk

$^1/_2$" dowel (15)"

craft knife

plastic stencil sheet

stencil crayons and brush

fabric protector spray

yarn, cording, or ribbon

*Put medical, diaper changing, or other items in the organizer
for babies. For toddlers, the organizer works well for storing
paint brushes, markers, glue, scissors, and varied craft supplies.*

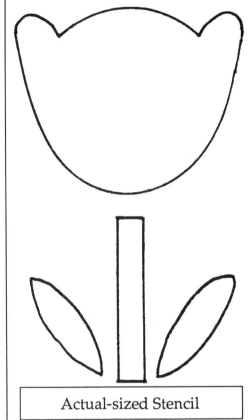

Actual-sized Stencil

1 Cut two 14"x 20" backings, one 5" x 14" top pocket, and one 6" x 14" bottom pocket from canvas. Hem one long side of both pockets.

2 Press lower edge of top pocket under $1/4$", and, with pocket bottom 9" above organizer bottom, topstitch to right side of backing. Baste bottom and sides of lower pocket to organizer bottom. Mark three vertical lines $3 1/2$" apart on top pocket and one vertical line dividing lower pocket in half. Topstitch lines to backing.

3 With right sides facing, sew backings together with $1/4$" seam allowance, leaving top edge open. Turn out. Press. Turn top edges under $1/4$" into opening. Topstitch across opening.

4 Turn top of organizer 2" to back and topstitch. Insert dowel.

5 Cut stencil. Stencil organizer, matching upper and lower flower colors. Cut a $1/4$" line border stencil the width of organizer and stencil line 2" above each pocket. Spray with fabric protector. Tie yarn or other material to dowel for hanging.

Delete dowel opening and make a flap to hang organizer over crib end.

✳ clothes ✳ rack ✳

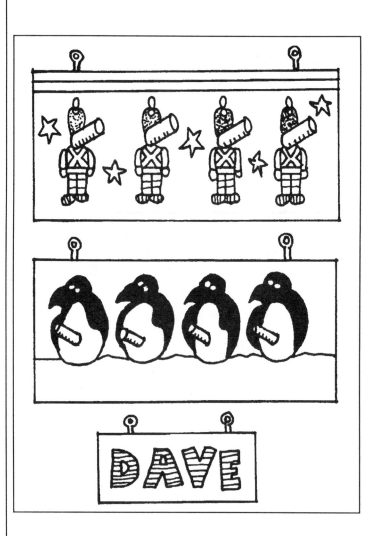

MATERIALS

1" x 6" pine board (15")

1" x 2 1/8" dowel screws – shaker pegs with built-in screws (4)

sandpaper

paint

1 1/8" screw eyes (2)

✳ ✳ ✳ ✳ ✳ ✳ ✳

1 Sand board edges.

2 Paint background color on rack.

3 Trace designs to rack and paint.

4 Screw dowels 3" apart and 3" from sides.

5 Screw eyes into top for hanging.

✳ ✳ ✳ ✳ ✳ ✳ ✳

Paint child's name on rack, stencil designs, or use hooks instead of dowel screws to vary rack.

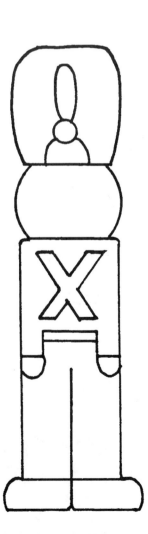

Actual-sized Designs

* picture * frame *

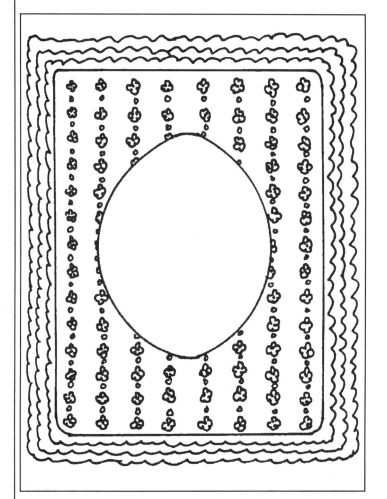

MATERIALS

matboard with pre-cut opening

cotton (to cover frame)

scissors

batting (same size as matboard)

ruler

glue

pre-gathered lace or eyelet ruffle

clothespins

nylon braided cording (2")

* * * * * * *

Densely patterned fabric prints look nice on frames!

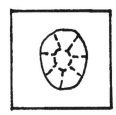

Cut inner opening and slits.

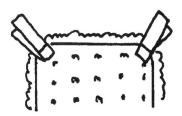

Use clothespins as clamps.

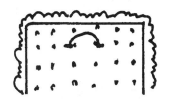

Sew cording to frame for hanger.

1 Place matboard on wrong side of fabric and cut fabric 1/2" larger on all sides than board. Cut batting and board backing same size as board.

2 Trace photo opening on fabric. Draw a line 1/2" inside of opening. Cut out inner opening and make slits 1/2" apart to outer outline for oval openings; corner slits for rectangle openings.

3 Place batting with cut-out opening on board, and glue excess fabric to wrong side of board. Cover backing like front, deleting batting.

4 With lace (lace length is equal to the sum of board sides) between boards, glue frame front and back together along sides and bottom. Leave frame top edges unglued for photograph insertion. Glue lace along top edge behind front frame piece. Clamp with clothespins while drying.

5 Sew cording loop to back in frame middle 3/4" from top.

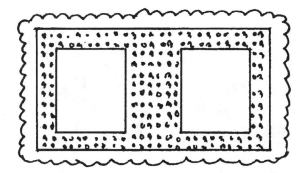

Cut your own mat from matboard using a craft knife. Common photograph sizes are 3 1/2" x 5", 5" x 7", or 8" x 10". Make more than one frame opening to display extra pictures.

✻ growth ✻ chart ✻

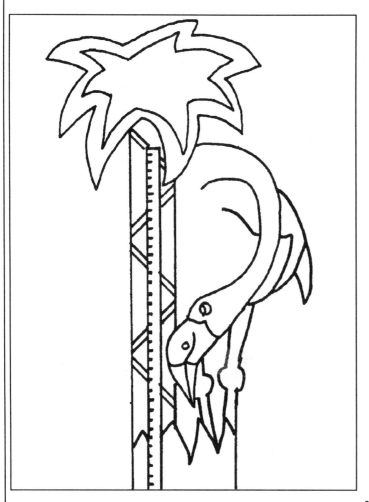

MATERIALS

$1/8$" standard hardboard (4' x 8')

saw

sandpaper

paint

dressmaker's tape measure (60")

glue

polyurethane sealant

✻ ✻ ✻ ✻ ✻ ✻ ✻

Nail chart to wall or inner door. Cut chart from foam board with a craft knife for a less heavy chart!

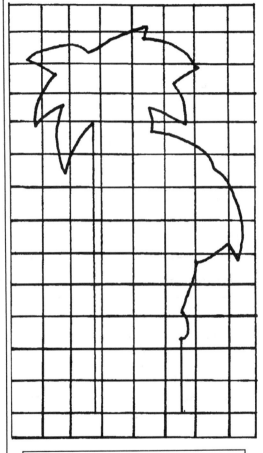

one square = 6"

1 Trace pattern to smooth side of board.

2 Cut shape from board. Sand any rough edges.

3 Paint a base coat of white. Use black paint to make outline shapes of flamingo, tree, and grass. Paint flamingo pink, beak tip black, remaining beak light pink or yellow, grass green, trunk tan or light brown, outer tree top dark green, inner tree top light green, and space above grass light blue.

4 Glue tape measure to tree. If tape is wrinkled, iron tape on low heat setting.

5 Seal chart with polyurethane, if desired.

✳ ✳ ✳ ✳ ✳ ✳ ✳

If you don't want to use a tape measure, paint or stencil numbers on tree trunk.

* door * guard *

MATERIALS

$1/2$" interior plywood (9" x 6 $1/2$")

1" interior plywood (5 $3/4$" x 1 $1/4$")

carbon paper

saw

sandpaper

wood glue

#4 $7/8$" woodscrews (2)

#6 1$1/4$" woodscrews (1)

paint

polyurethane sealant

✳ ✳ ✳ ✳ ✳ ✳ ✳

Door guards (inserted under doors' bottom edges) prevent doors from being closed. They are also attractive wooden sculptures in their own right.

Cut outline and feet.

Screw dragon to stand.

1 Enlarge dragon illustration (on facing page) by 35%. Trace enlarged dragon outline over carbon paper to $1/2$" wood piece. Trace lower dragon feet, which will stand out in relief, on separate section of $1/2$" wood.

2 Cut outline and the two oval feet with saw. Cut dragon stand from 1" wood piece. (Illustration of stand below is actual-size.)

3 Sand all edges. Glue bottom feet to dragon front, and use one $7/8$" screw to attach each foot to front.

4 Center, glue, and screw the 1" square section of the stand to the bottom edge of the dragon's back. The angled stand side goes under the door while the flat side is on the floor.

5 Paint the dragon using vivid colors, such as pink and green, and paint detailing accents (wings, stomach, foot pads, head scales, and tail). Seal with polyurethane.

✳ ✳ ✳ ✳ ✳ ✳ ✳

Stand — Actual-size

* nursery * wreath *

MATERIALS

12" rattan or grapevine wreath

pre-cut wooden hearts with holes (5)

pastel blue and pink paint

$1/8$" white ribbon (1 yd.)

$1/8$" pastel blue ribbon (1 $2/3$ yds.)

$1/8$" pastel pink ribbon (2 yds.)

ruler

scissors

dried baby's breath flowers

* * * * * * *

Mix white paint with a small bit of red paint for pink and with blue paint for pastel blue!

Knot ribbons behind hearts.

1 Leave wreath natural-colored or spray paint it. Paint three blue and two pink hearts.

2 Cut three 12" pink ribbons and two 12" blue ribbons. Thread ribbons through contrasting heart holes, and knot center of ribbons behind hearts.

3 Tie ribbons to wreath with a double knot.

Use ribbon to make center bow.

4 Take leaves off flower stems. Weave 3 1/2" stems into wreath.

5 Use white and left-over pink and blue ribbons to tie a bow at the top of the wreath's center. Hang wreath on nail in wall.

*Other cut-out wood shapes
such as bears, houses, or rocking horses,
could be substituted for hearts.
And baby's breath can be spray painted
if you are using a different color scheme.*

Take leaves off flower stems.

✳ wall ✳ hanging ✳

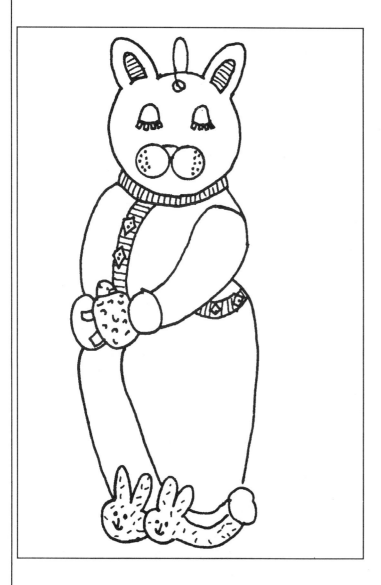

MATERIALS

white flour (4 cups)

water (1½ cups)

salt (1 cup)

rolling pin

knife

cookie tray

sharp pointed object

paint

polyurethane sealant

✳ ✳ ✳ ✳ ✳ ✳ ✳

*Use left-over dough for
Christmas ornaments or
decorations to hang in front
of window in child's room.*

I*N*S*T*R*U*C*T*I*O*N*S

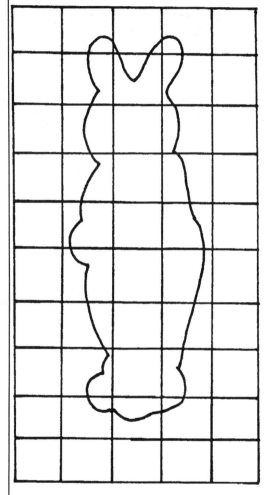

one square = 2"

1 Mix all ingredients, and knead five minutes. Roll out dough with rolling pin to $\frac{1}{4}$" thickness.

2 Using pattern, cut rabbit shape with knife, and place on cookie sheet. Add detailing (stuffed lamb, facial features, hands, pajama ribbing, and slippers) by pressing dough bits to shape. Dampen rabbit and detailing before pressing together. Smooth detailing edges.

3 Use ice pick, nail, or other sharp object to make hole for hanging.

4 Bake in 200 degree oven until rabbit is firm, golden, and back is hard.

5 Paint rabbit front detailing, paint back a solid color, and seal.

✳ ✳ ✳ ✳ ✳ ✳ ✳

* switch * plate *

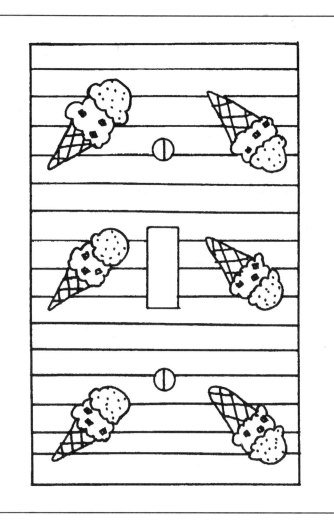

MATERIALS

switch plate

medium-weight cotton fabric

scissors

ruler

glue

❋ ❋ ❋ ❋ ❋ ❋ ❋

Coordinate plate fabric with nursery colors and patterns!

I*N*S*T*R*U*C*T*I*O*N*S

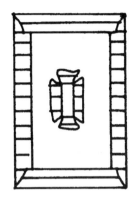

Glue fabric to plate inside.

1 Lay plate on wrong side of fabric, and cut fabric 1/2" larger on all sides.

2 Glue fabric to front with liquid glue or stick glue. Use liquid glue to glue fabric edges to back side of plate.

3 Make vertical slit in switch opening with scissors. Cut four slits from vertical slit to corners of switch opening.

4 Glue excess opening fabric to back side of plate. Secure with tape, if necessary, to dry.

5 Use scissors to pierce a small hole at screw openings. Insert screws.

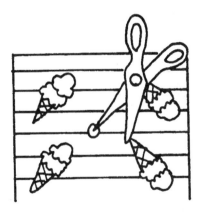

Pierce screw holes with scissors.

✳ ✳ ✳ ✳ ✳ ✳ ✳

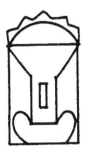

Make your own switch plate by cutting a balsa wood plate and painting it. You can cut the balsa larger than the plate and have projecting parts, such as balloons rising above top edge.

✻ family ✻ tree ✻

MATERIALS

½" interior plywood (19" x 14½")

white paint

craft knife

stencil plastic sheet

pastel stencil paint or crayons

ruler

carbon paper

¾" embossed pine molding (2¼ yds.)

1" panel nails (about 14)

black paint

✽ ✽ ✽ ✽ ✽ ✽ ✽

You can use wooden hearts or other shapes in different sizes instead of stencils. If necessary, adjust wooden heart measurements with wood background dimensions before attaching hearts with glue.

I * N * S * T * R * U * C * T * I * O * N * S

1 Thoroughly sand wood to remove roughness. Paint front, back, and sides of wood with two coats of white paint.

2 Using diagrams, cut heart stencils with knife and plastic sheet.

3 Stencil hearts to board. Leave equal margins on all sides. All rows are 1" apart. Leave 1/8" between great-grandparents; 2" apart for grandparents; and 6" apart for parents. Trace houses with carbon paper on lower left and right corners, and paint.

4 Print names of family members with black paint on hearts. Add birth years, if desired.

5 Cut and nail embossed molding to board sides. Attach screw eyes and picture wire or self-leveling saw tooth picture hangers to board for hanging.

✳ ✳ ✳ ✳ ✳ ✳ ✳

Use leaves or other motifs instead of hearts.

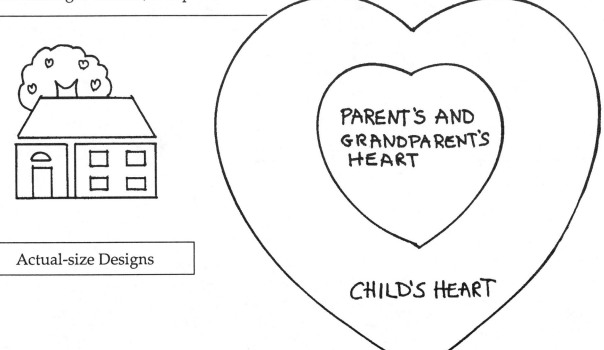

Actual-size Designs

PARENT'S AND GRANDPARENT'S HEART

CHILD'S HEART

sampler

MATERIALS

10" decorative embroidery hoop

disappearing tracing paper
(at fabric store)

gingham cotton (12" x 12")

18 count cross stitch cotton
(4 1/2" x 4 1/2")

embroidery floss

glue

1/2" pre-gathered ruffle (2/3 yd.)

1" pre-gathered ruffle (1 yd.)

❊ ❊ ❊ ❊ ❊ ❊ ❊

*◊ If you are uneasy about your embroidery skills,
then substitute a marker or paintbrush for needle and thread.
Test the marker on a fabric scrap
to make sure it doesn't "bleed" on fabric.*

Cut excess material from back.

1 Pencil the child's name, birthdate, and weight (in $1/2$" high letters and numbers) with tracing paper on the cross stitch fabric. Or use removable embroidery tissue paper instead of pencil outlines.

2 Embroider information using the outline stitch or cross stitch. Use a small embroidery hoop to hold fabric, if necessary.

3 Stretch background gingham over hoop. Cut excess fabric from sampler back.

4 Glue embroidered information square to middle of covered hoop. Glue or sew $1/2$" ruffle around raw edges of square.

5 Glue 1" ruffle to hoop back over trimmed fabric edges.

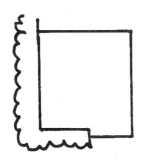

Begin attaching $1/2$" ruffle at information square bottom middle.

Instead of making a sampler, stretch a lace panel with nursery design over solid-colored fabric on hoop.

❋ bookends ❋

If you want to make wooden bookends instead of using metal bookends, here's how: Cut a 1" x 6" (1$\frac{1}{4}$') pine, oak or other board into two 6$\frac{1}{2}$" x 5$\frac{1}{2}$" backs and two 7" x 5$\frac{1}{2}$" bottoms. Glue and screw each pair together with 5$\frac{1}{2}$" sides together.

MATERIALS

1$\frac{1}{4}$" wood blocks with letters (14)

metal bookends (2)

spray paint

wood glue

polyurethane spray sealant

❋

INSTRUCTIONS

1 Glue each block tier separately; then glue tiers together.

2 Spray paint bookends. Paint block sides, if desired.

3 Glue block stack to bookends.

4 Spray bookends and blocks with sealant.

❋ ❋ ❋ ❋ ❋ ❋ ❋

• 3 •

Playtime

• noah's • ark •

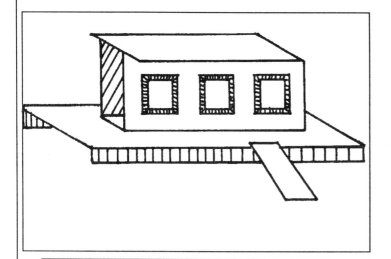

MATERIALS

½" interior plywood (2' x 4')

pencil

ruler

saw

1" finishing nails (about 35)

wood glue

carbon paper

sandpaper

paint or stain

polyurethane sealant

♥ ♥ ♥ ♥ ♥ ♥ ♥

INSTRUCTIONS

1 Cut two 7" x 5" house sides; one 5" x 5" house back; one 8" x 7" roof; one 10" x 14" ark base; two 1" x 10" ark supports; and one 5 ½" x 3" ramp.

2 Glue and nail house back between sides; centered, overlapping roof to sides; completed house to base; and base to supports.

3 Sand ark. Stain, or paint ark and detailing, such as windows. Seal.

4 Trace animal block shapes to wood with carbon paper.

5 Cut, sand, paint, and seal animal blocks.

♥ two-sided ♥ doll ♥

MATERIALS

medium-weight fabric for body (1/3 yd.)

varied fabric scraps for clothing

yarn

scissors

thread

iron

embroidery floss

This doll, which is awake and wearing a dress on one side and asleep in a nightgown on the other, will fit comfortably into doll bed in this book. Clothing for each side should be appropriate and distinctly different for maximum authenticity.

♥

I ♥ N ♥ S ♥ T ♥ R ♥ U ♥ C ♥ T ♥ I ♥ O ♥ N ♥ S

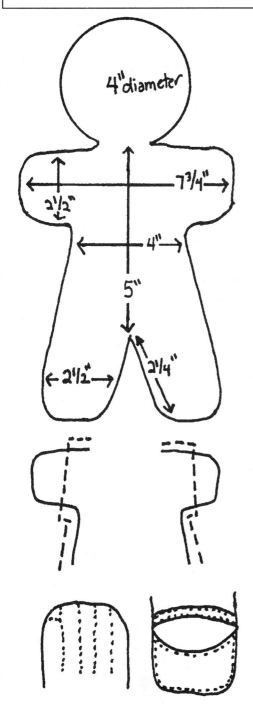

4" diameter

7³/₄"

2¹/₂"

4"

5"

2¹/₂"

2¹/₄"

1. Use diagram for pattern, and cut two doll shapes from body fabric and enough 1¹/₂" yarn pieces to circle head.

2. Sew yarn ends to head on one side with other yarn ends pointing to center. With right sides facing, sew shapes together with ¹/₄" seam allowance, leaving a 3" opening on doll side. Turn out. Press. Stuff. Slipstitch opening closed.

3. Embroider facial details as shown in illustration.

4. To make dress/nightgown, cut two fabric dress shapes ¹/₂" wider than doll body. With right sides facing, sew corresponding shoulders and sides together with ¹/₄" seam allowance. Turn out. Press.

5. Hem sleeve openings and bottom edges. Decorate clothing with ribbons, lace, or other materials.

Sew fingers by topstitching through hands.
Use felt scraps to make shoes or even ballet slippers on each doll side.

• doll • bed •

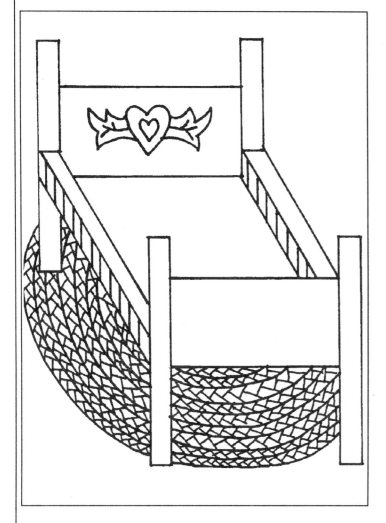

MATERIALS

1" x 8" pine board (6')

$1/4$" interior plywood for mattress support (12" x 17$3/4$")

saw

wood glue

#4 1$1/2$" wood screws (12)

$3/4$" brads or finishing nails (8)

sandpaper

wood stain

polyurethane sealant

♥ ♥ ♥ ♥ ♥ ♥ ♥

The doll mattress, blanket, and doll pillow with pillow case in this book are sized for this bed, as is the two-sided doll.

♥

I ♥ N ♥ S ♥ T ♥ R ♥ U ♥ C ♥ T ♥ I ♥ O ♥ N ♥ S

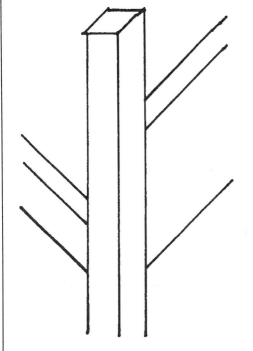

1 Cut two 14" x 1" headboard posts; two 11" x 1" endboard posts; one 7" x 10" headboard; one $4\frac{1}{2}$" x 10" endboard; and two $17\frac{3}{4}$" x 1" side rails.

2 Glue and screw pieces together except for plywood mattress support.

3 Nail mattress support to side rails.

4 Sand, stain, and seal wood.

Sides and bed ends are 4" above ground.

Use a wood chisel, woodburner, or stencil to make a headboard decoration before attaching bed pieces. Or cut beveled edge design into headboard and footboard.

♥ doll ♥ bedding ♥

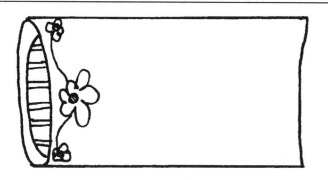

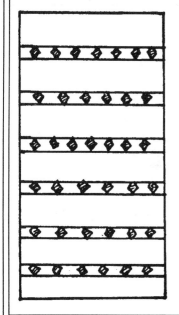

MATERIALS

pillow fabric ($1/6$ yd.)

pillow case fabric ($1/6$ yd.)

mattress fabric ($1/3$ yd.)

blanket fabric ($1/2$ yd.)

batting or stuffing

scissors

thread

iron

♥ ♥ ♥ ♥ ♥ ♥ ♥

Bedding will fit doll bed in This book!

Leave pillow case fold unsewn.

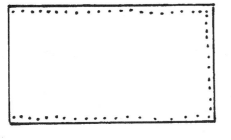

Leave one mattress side unsewn
for stuffing insertion.

1 Cut two 5 1/2" x 8" pillow pieces; one 6" x 18" pillow case; two 14" x 20" blanket pieces; and two 18 1/4" x 10 1/2" mattress pieces.

2 Pillow, blanket, and mattress: With right sides facing, sew all corresponding pieces together with a 1/4" seam allowance, leaving small opening to turn out.

3 Turn out. Press.

4 Insert batting or stuffing into pillow and mattress. Slip stitch pillow, mattress, and blanket openings.

5 Pillow case: Fold pillow case piece to measure 6" x 9". With right sides facing, sew top and bottom long side edges together with 1/4" seam allowance. Turn out. Press. Hem pillow case opening, and insert pillow.

Options: *Make a minature quilt instead of blanket. Stitch corresponding fabrics together for reversible blanket.*
Use 1/4" foam in mattress for extra firmness.
Sew lace to pillow case edges.

building ♥ blocks

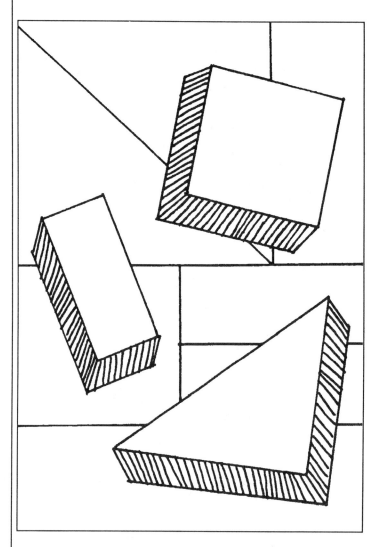

MATERIALS

1" x 10" pine board (10')

pencil

ruler

saw

sandpaper

*One board will make 72 blocks.
You may want to paint blocks in
bright colors and seal
with polyurethane or leave blocks
natural colored and seal.*

I ♥ N ♥ S ♥ T ♥ R ♥ U ♥ C ♥ T ♥ I ♥ O ♥ N ♥ S

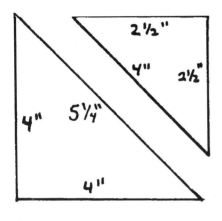

1 Draw block patterns on wood.
Position patterns for most efficient cutting.

2 Cut shapes from wood with saw.

3 Sand edges.

4 Paint or seal, if desired.

♥ ♥ ♥ ♥ ♥ ♥ ♥

*Cut a 1" dowel into 4" or 8" lengths
for column blocks.*

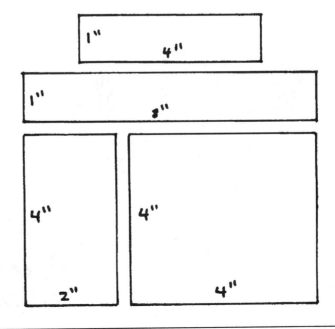

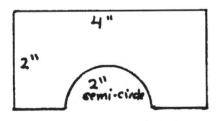

huggable ♥ bunnies

MATERIALS

adult-size nylon ankle sock with heel (1)

scissors

thread

polyester stuffing

embroidery floss

$1/8$" double-faced satin ribbon ($1/3$ yd.)

*Child-sized socks may be used
for smaller rabbits.
Create a family of bunnies
from different-sized socks.
Give bunny family
members special detailing, such as
a bonnet for mother, a bowtie
for father, a bib for baby,
ear ribbons for sister, and a cap
for brother*

I♥N♥S♥T♥R♥U♥C♥T♥I♥O♥N♥S

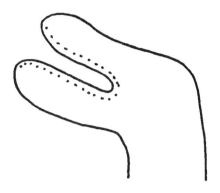

Sew cut toe section for ears.

1 Cut sock toe section in half (about 4") for ears, stopping about 3" from heel as shown on diagram.

2 With sock inside out, sew cut halves with a small seam into ears.

3 Stuff toy through sock leg opening. Baste around leg opening, and pull basting thread to close leg opening. Whipstitch together sides of gathered opening.

4 Embroider eyes and nose on heel section of sock using the satin stitch.

5 Tie ribbon around rabbit neck. Make a bow, and sew bow center to rabbit.

Sew bow to neck.

Securely sew pompom on back for cottontail if giving to an older child. Keep pompoms from younger children as pompoms may be dangerous if swallowed.

♥ christmas ♥ stocking ♥

MATERIALS

felt for stocking ($1/3$ yd.)

white felt (9" x 12")

felt scraps (assorted colors)

scissors

glue

embroidery floss

decorative notions such as sequins, rhinestones, satin, velvet

♥ ♥ ♥ ♥ ♥ ♥ ♥

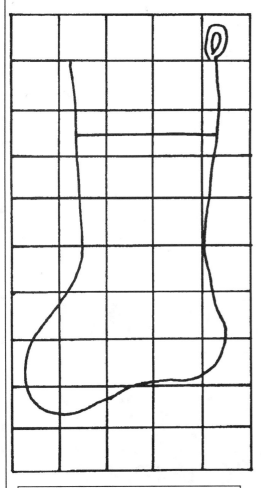

one square = 2"

1 Cut two stocking pieces from large felt piece and two top edgings from white felt using diagram. Cut out felt shapes for decorations and letters for name. For extra specialness, use child's interests to personalize stocking.

2 Glue shapes to stocking front and letters to front edging. (Sew sequins or glass beads on decorations for extra highlights.)

3 With wrong sides facing, sew stocking pieces together with whipstitch or blanket stitch.

4 Sew white edging together on sides and to stocking.

5 Cut a 2" x 1/2" felt stocking hanger. Loop hanger and sew to upper right-hand corner.

♥ ♥ ♥ ♥ ♥ ♥ ♥

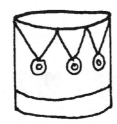

♥ soft ♥ rattles ♥

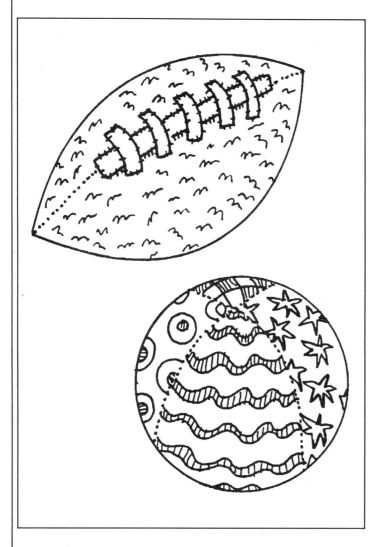

MATERIALS

fleece or other soft fabric ($1/8$ yd.)

scissors

thread

polyester stuffing

child-proof empty vial (5 dram size)

dried beans (16)

white felt for football lacings

♥ ♥ ♥ ♥ ♥ ♥ ♥

Get empty, childproof pill vial from a pharmacy!

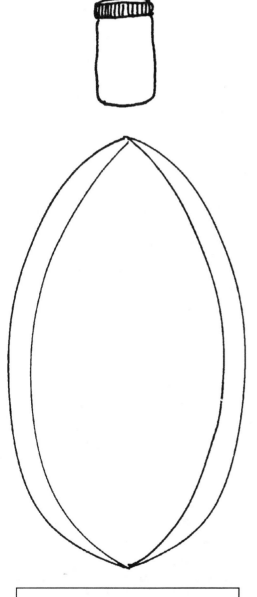

1 Using adjoining patterns, cut four of inner outline shape for football or four of outer outline for ball.

2 With right sides facing, sew each side to another side using a $1/4$" seam allowance, leaving $2 1/2$" of ending seam unsewn. Turn out. Stuff.

3 Put beans in vial. Screw lid securely, and insert into ball middle. Adjust stuffing to thoroughly cover vial.

4 Slipstitch opening closed.

5 Cut one 3" x $1/4$" felt strip and five 1" x $1/4$" felt lacings for football. Sew pieces to football with strip on an outer seam.

Use four different colored, patterned, or textured fabrics for ball sections. Textured fabrics will introduce child to varying tactile sensations.

Actual-size Patterns

♥ puppets ♥

MATERIALS

heavy-weight fabric such as corduroy, wool, fake fur (1/3 yd.)

ruler

scissors

thread

decorations (felt, buttons, braid, plastic eyes)

*Puppets
may be used to teach children
good behavior, such as sharing.
Give a whole set of puppets as a gift
to toddler to encourage role-playing,
observation and imitative behaviors.
Or
make puppets of all the characters in a
story and give a gift of the book plus
the puppet characters.*

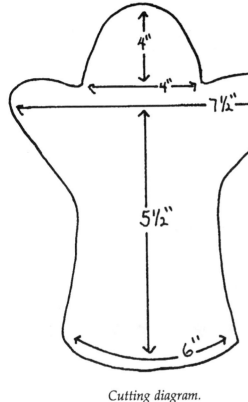

Cutting diagram.

1 Cut two fabric pieces of basic shape as shown on diagram for each puppet.

2 With right sides facing, sew sides and tops together with 1/4" seam allowance. Turn out.

3 Hem bottom opening.

4 Decorate extensively with sewing notions so characters are very obvious.

♥ ♥ ♥ ♥ ♥ ♥ ♥

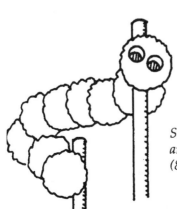

Sew six 1" pompoms together and attach to two 1/2" dowels (8" long) for a moving worm.

♥ monkey ♥ toy ♥

MATERIALS

work socks with contrasting toe and heel (1 pair)

scissors

thread

polyester stuffing

blue and red embroidery floss

*Make a t-shirt
for monkey using clothing instructions
for "Two-Sided Doll."*

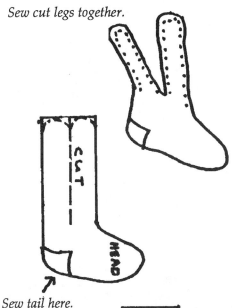

Sew cut legs together.

Sew tail here.

1 Cut monkey pieces using diagram.

2 Cut leg opening as shown. With right sides facing, sew each leg together, leaving an opening at crotch. Turn monkey out, and stuff through crotch. Whipstitch crotch opening.

3 With right sides facing, sew corresponding arm, ears, and tail pieces together with a narrow seam, leaving open sides to connect to monkey. Stuff tail and arms, and whipstitch these and unstuffed ears to monkey.

4 Whipstitch muzzle to face, stuffing while you sew.

5 Use satin stitch for eyes, running stitch for mouth, and knots for nostrils.

♥ ♥ ♥ ♥ ♥ ♥ ♥

Make several identical or differently-adorned monkeys. Sew together at hands, and hang monkey chain for a wall decoration.

fruitface ♥ puzzle

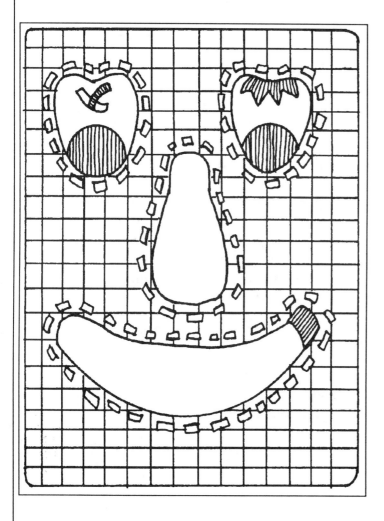

MATERIALS

cardboard – 8 1/2" x 11" (2)

fabric (1/3 yd.)

batting (8 1/2" x 11")

ruler

scissors

glue

clothespins

pink, red, green, and yellow felt

polyester stuffing

embroidery floss

2" Velcro (7")

Fruits attach to puzzle board with Velcro. You can use this same fastening technique for other and larger puzzles, such as varied color felt squares to create designs, a flower divided into sections, or farm yard animals with a barn in the background. ♥

PINK

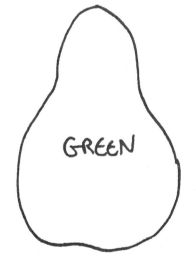

GREEN

1 Cut two 10 1/2" x 13" fabric pieces and one 8 1/2" x 11" batting piece. Place batting on one cardboard piece to make the puzzle front, and cover batting with right side of fabric facing out. Glue fabric edges to back of board. Cover second board with fabric only for the back of the puzzle.

2 With cardboard sides facing, glue fabric-covered boards together. Clamp sides with clothespins while drying.

3 Enlarge fruit patterns 35%, and cut two of each shape. Stuff and sew corresponding fruit shapes together using running stitch or whipstitch. Sew fruit accents, such as the apple stem, to fruits. Add white circles for eyes to apple and strawberry, if you want, or white rectangles for teeth to the banana.

4 Embroider fruit outlines on front board (the one with batting.)

5 Cut Velcro strip in two 1 1/2" sections for apple and strawberry shapes and two 2" sections for pear nose and banana mouth. Sew one strip to each fruit and also to corresponding fruit outline on board.

RED

YELLOW

♥ toy ♥ box ♥

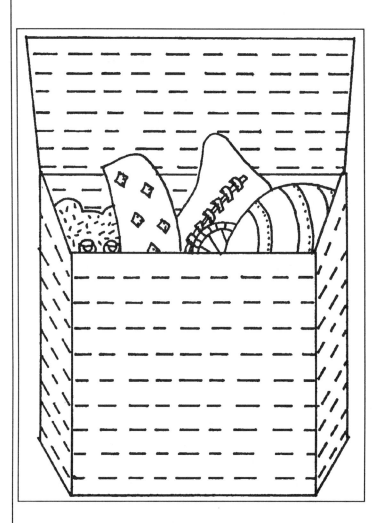

MATERIALS

cotton ($7/8$ yd.)

ruler

scissors

thread

iron

$1/2$" foam (21" x 28")

This is a container for small toys. Use it in the car, playpen, and other locations for storage and to play with infants who like to hide and retrieve toys. You might even want to put a handle on sides for carrying.

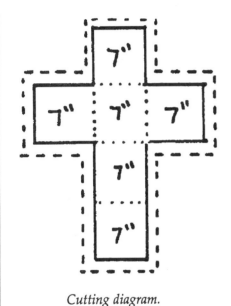

Cutting diagram.

1 Cut two fabric pieces ¼" larger on all sides than six-square area. Cut foam the exact dimensions as diagrammed six-square area. (Make a larger box by increasing size of each square, such as 10" squares.)

2 Press outer fabric edges ¼" to wrong side. Place foam between fabric box pieces with wrong sides facing. Topstitch along all side edges to connect pieces.

3 Draw 7" square division lines on one side of fabric. Topstitch over these lines.

4 With right sides facing, sew bottom to sides and sides to sides with ¼" seam allowances to make a box.

5 Turn out. Box top will be attached to only one side.

♥ ♥ ♥ ♥ ♥ ♥ ♥

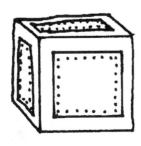

Topstitch contrasting 5" fabric squares to all box sides before sewing foam and fabric together. Sew or glue appliques to each square.

♥ easter ♥ basket ♥

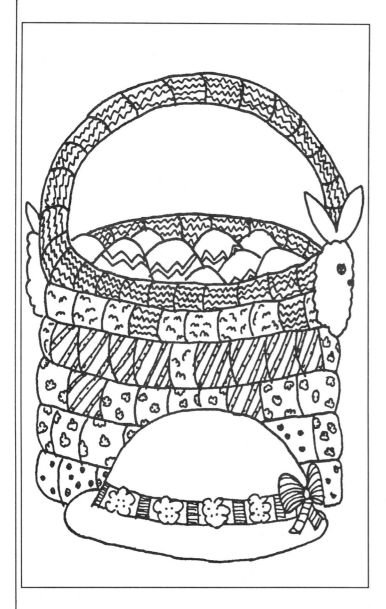

MATERIALS

1/2" rope or polyester craft coiling (26')

medium-weight cotton (3 1/2 yds.)

scissors

thread

♥ ♥ ♥ ♥ ♥ ♥ ♥

Use different patterned cottons for a colorful basket!

I♥N♥S♥T♥R♥U♥C♥T♥I♥O♥N♥S

Figure eight tie: Wrap strip halfway around coiling, then wrap strip below to coiling on preceding round and bring back to original coiling point as if making the number eight.

1 Tear or cut fabric into 1" wide strips. Make strips as long as possible. Join fabric strips by seam or knotting as needed.

2 To wrap basket bottom: Wrap a strip around rope end four times, overlapping each wrap. Coil wrapped rope, and join coiling together with figure eight tie to form base.

3 Continue wrapping and securing coiling to earlier rounds with figure eight tie every four wraps.

4 When the bottom has a 7" diameter, continue wrapping rope and place rope rows on top of each other (using figure eight tie to secure rows) to form the 4 1/2" vertical basket sides.

5 To make basket handles: Use figure eight tie four times to secure and end basket coiling. Wrap rope for 14", and secure to other side with four figure eight ties.

Sew fake fur rabbit faces to sides. To make rabbit face, cut an oval, fold it in half length-wise, and whipstitch oval sides together. Use buttons for eyes and nose. Repeat steps for second face.

FOLD

birth ♥ scrapbook

MATERIALS

iron

medium-weight fabric

scrapbook or photo album

scissors

glue

masking tape

lace cotton doily

heat transfer letters

spray adhesive

Items to put in a scrapbook:
family tree; picture of pregnant mother and expectant father and siblings; picture of parents and siblings as infants; hospital picture; news headlines on date of birth; hospital bill; vital statistics; news clipping of birth; description of first home; list of congratulatory phone calls, presents, and visitors; picture of baby's room; and other information.

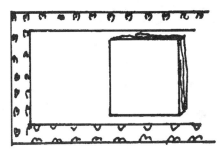

Place book on fabric.

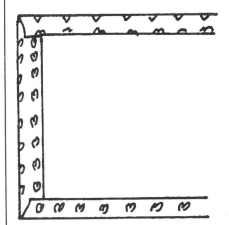

Glue borders to inside of book.

1 Press fabric. Open album and place on wrong side of fabric. Add 2" to all album sides, and cut fabric. (If you want to make a plusher scrapbook, place a layer of thick batting between fabric and book. Cut batting same size as book cover.)

2 Press under all edges of fabric $1/4$" to wrong fabric side.

3 Use tape to position fabric borders to inner album. Cut small slits at each side of album spine to aid in gluing. Glue borders as if wrapping a package.

4 Use heat transfer letters or embroidery floss to spell out child's name on doily.

5 Spray doily lightly with adhesive, and attach to front cover.

♥ ♥ ♥ ♥ ♥ ♥ ♥

Cut and glue a felt design or pre-embroidered thick ribbon to cover instead of doily.

♥ sandbox ♥

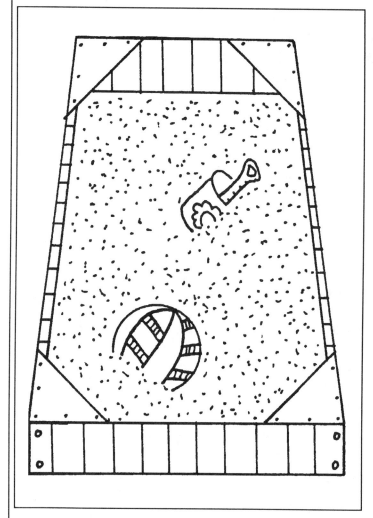

MATERIALS

2" x 10" outdoor treated pine boards
for the box – $4\frac{1}{2}$' (4)

$3\frac{1}{2}$" x $\frac{3}{8}$" lag screws (8)

1" x 10" outdoor treated pine boards
for seats – $1\frac{3}{4}$' (2)

saw

#6 3" wood screws (20)

sand

*Use discarded kitchen utensils,
such as muffin tins, sieves, measuring
spoons, or plastic cups for sand toys.*

I♥N♥S♥T♥R♥U♥C♥T♥I♥O♥N♥S

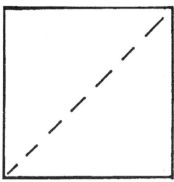

Cut seats from squares.

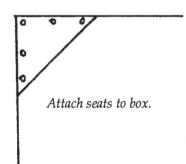

Attach seats to box.

1 Join board ends to form square with two lag screws holding each junction.

2 Cut crossboard seats by diagonally cutting a 10" square from 1" x 10" to make two seats. Repeat diagonal cut on remaining squared board for two more seats.

3 Attach seats to box with five woodscrews for each seat. Sink screw heads as far as possible into seats so heads don't catch on clothing.

4 Fill box with sand.

Attach a $^1/_2$" plywood sheet with woodscrews to box for a bottom. A bottom will keep dirt from sand, but will not drain water.

• stick • horse •

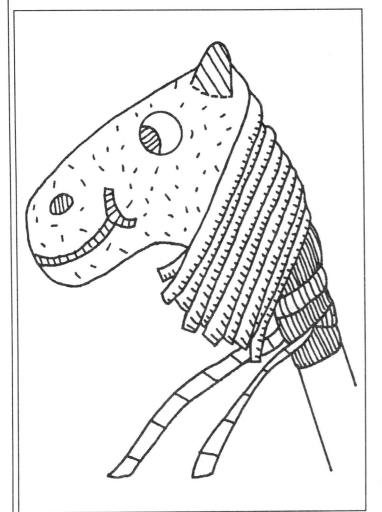

MATERIALS

1" dowel (30")

man's work sock with heel (1)

polyester stuffing

glue

bicycle cloth handlebar tape or duct tape

scissors

knit-fabric strips – $1/2$" x 5" (16)

felt scraps for facial details

braided cord for reins (1 yd.)

♥ ♥ ♥ ♥ ♥ ♥ ♥

Instead of a dowel, use an old broomstick!

I ♥ N ♥ S ♥ T ♥ R ♥ U ♥ C ♥ T ♥ I ♥ O ♥ N ♥ S

Wrap excess sock around dowel.

1 Stuff sock except for last 3" on leg opening.

2 Insert dowel and adjust stuffing. Wrap excess sock material around dowel. Wrap tape around wrapped sock. Catch cord ends in tape. Continue wrapping tape several times to secure sock and cord ends.

3 Cut two felt diamonds for ears. Fold in half. Stuff. Sew ear sides with right sides facing, and sew to head.

4 Turn mane strip ends under and sew below sock heel on both sides of mane part.

5 Glue or sew felt nostril and eye ovals on. Embroider smile with outline stitch.

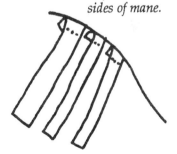

Sew mane strips on both sides of mane.

♥ ♥ ♥ ♥ ♥ ♥ ♥

Sew and stuff a horn between ears to make a stick unicorn.

wooden ♥ soldiers

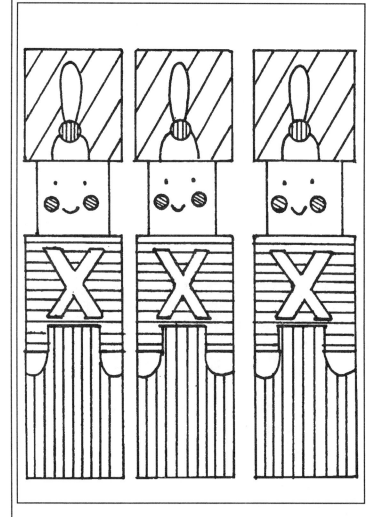

♥ ♥ ♥ ♥ ♥ ♥ ♥

A miter box and saw are good for cutting dowels.

♥

MATERIALS

1" dowel – 36" (2)

$3/4$" dowel – 36" (1)

saw

sandpaper

wood glue

polyurethane sealant

INSTRUCTIONS

1 Cut $3/4$" head lengths from smaller dowel.

2 Bodies ($2\,1/2$") and hats ($1\,1/4$") are cut from 1" dowel

3 Sand rough edges.

4 Stack, center, and glue dowels.

5 Paint. Seal

• 4 •

Sleep, Little One, Sleep

nap • sign

ANNA'S
SLEEPING

MATERIALS

felt for sign background (9" x 12")

paper

felt (assorted colors)

scissors

glue

$1/2$" dowel (12)

yard, cording, or ribbon for hanging ties

Use sign to help babies and toddlers to sleep free of disturbances, and to help older children feel special at rest time.

INSTRUCTIONS

NAP ZONE

1 Use your imagination, and design your own nap sign. Draw designs on paper and cut out designs for patterns.

2 Cut felt designs and arrange on background. Sign measures 9" horizontally. Glue inner edges of felt pieces to background piece when sure of placement. (You can make a modified soft sculpture sign by inserting a small amount of stuffing under some of the larger felt pieces before completing gluing.)

3 Fold top edge of large felt piece 3/4" to back.

4 Glue edge bottom to sign, and insert dowel.

5 Tie yarn, string, cording, or ribbon to dowel ends to hang sign on door knob.

John is Resting

Nap in Progress

Reading Time

Shhhh I'm Resting

child's quilt

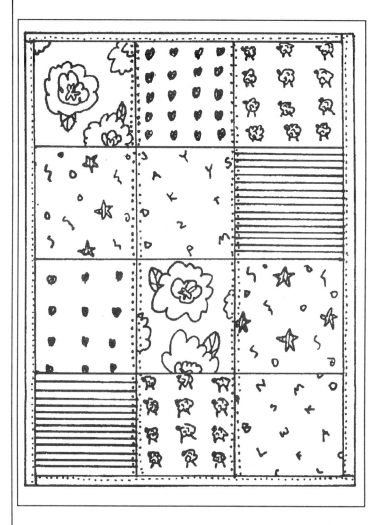

MATERIALS

medium-weight fabric for quilt back
(1 1/3 yds.)

medium-weight cotton in assorted
patterns and colors for quilt squares
(1 1/3 yds.)

quilt batting – 45" width (1 1/3 yds.)

scissors

thread

double-fold bias tape (5 yds.)

*Use child-motif
or solid color fabrics for quilt squares.
Or sew appliques on each square.*

I❀N❀S❀T❀R❀U❀C❀T❀I❀O❀N❀S

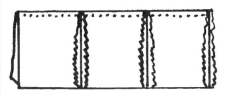

Sew squares to form rows.

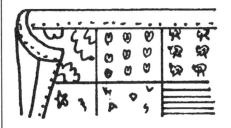

Cut bias tape to fit borders.

1 Cut twelve 12"-squares from assorted patterns and one 35" x 46$\frac{1}{2}$" backing. Use a cardboard template to mark designs, if desired.

2 With right sides facing, sew three squares together cross-wise with $\frac{1}{4}$" seam allowance. Make four of these rows. Sew the four three-square rows together length-wise with right sides facing and $\frac{1}{4}$" seam allowance. Press seams.

3 With wrong sides facing and batting between blocks and quilt backing, topstitch on each side of front vertical seams to connect backing to quilt blocks.

4 Insert quilt into bias tape fold, and sew tape around all sides.

Cut smaller squares for a less bold quilt. You'll need forty-eight for a 6"-square quilt or one hundred and eight for a 4"-square quilt! You can also tie-off the quilt with knots placed in the square middles or corners using a needle threaded with yarn or heavy thread instead of topstitching.

tooth · fairy · pillow

MATERIALS

light or medium-weight fabric (1/6 yd.)

ruler

scissors

iron

embroidery floss

pre-gathered lace (3/4 ft.)

straight pins

polyester stuffing

*Put pillow with freshly
lost tooth under bed pillow
at night for best results.*

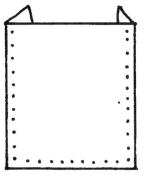

Topstitch pocket to pillow.

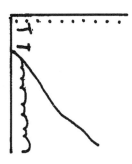

Lace faces inward while seaming.

1 Cut two $7^3/4$" x $5^1/4$" pillow pieces and one $2^1/4$" x $2^1/2$" pocket.

2 Embroider name and words on right side of one piece. Narrowly hem one $2^1/2$" edge of pocket piece for top opening. Press edges of pocket sides and bottom $1/4$" to wrong side, and topstitch edges to embroidered pillow piece $3/4$" from left border and $1^1/2$" from top.

3 With right sides facing, and lace pointing inward between pieces, sew pillow together with a $1/4$" seam allowance, leaving a 2" opening.

4 Turn out. Press.

5 Lightly stuff pillow. Slipstitch opening closed.

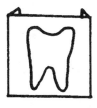

Embroider a tooth with outline stitch on pocket.

crib • bumper

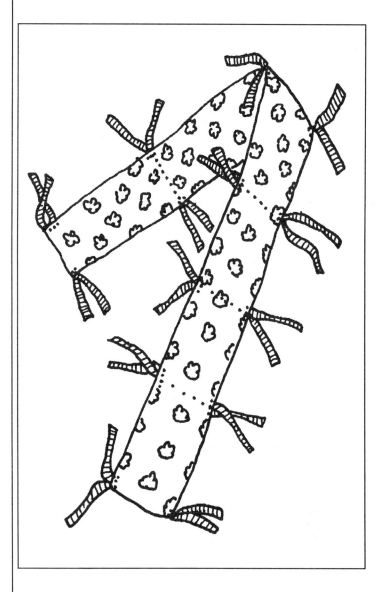

MATERIALS

medium-weight cotton (2$\frac{1}{4}$ yd.)

ruler

scissors

quilt batting – 96" width (1$\frac{1}{3}$ yds.)

thread

iron

$\frac{1}{2}$" ribbon (7 yds.)

Crib dimensions vary.
Measure crib for best fit.
For a special gift, give crib bumpers
and matching crib ruffle
and/or coverlet.

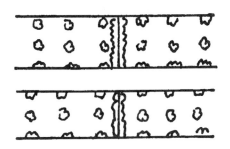

Sew four pieces to make bumper front and back.

1 Cut four 11" x 79" cotton pieces and four batting pieces of the same measurement.

2 With right sides facing, sew ends of two cotton pieces together to measure 11" x 157$\frac{1}{2}$". Sew together ends of the two other cotton pieces.

3 With two layers of batting pinned to wrong side of one long cotton piece and right sides facing, sew both cotton pieces together with a $\frac{1}{4}$" seam allowance to form one long bumper, leaving one short end open. Turn out. Slipstitch opening closed.

4 Measure six equal sections on bumper. Topstitch vertical lines through all thicknesses, making six sections.

5 Cut ribbon into 18" pieces, and sew ribbon centers to top and bottom of each topstitched line and at bumper ends.

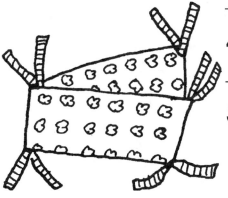

Sew ties to upper and lower edges of top-stitched lines.

Use $\frac{1}{4}$" or $\frac{1}{2}$" foam instead of batting.

❀

❀ crib ❀ dust ❀ ruffle ❀

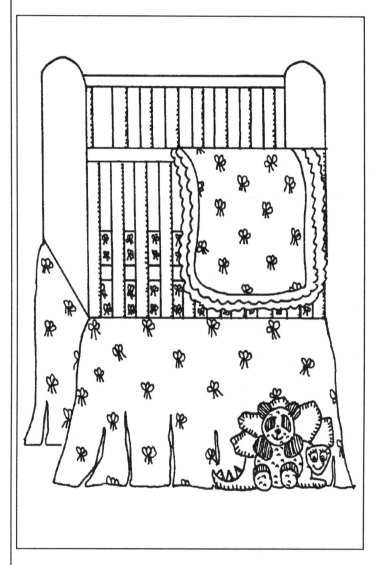

MATERIALS

cotton fabric

ruler

scissors

thread

*Ruffle top
is placed between box springs
and crib mattress.*

I ❀ N ❀ S ❀ T ❀ R ❀ U ❀ C ❀ T ❀ I ❀ O ❀ N ❀ S

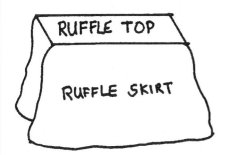

Cut three sections for ruffle.

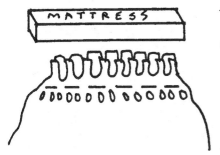

Gather skirts' top edges to equal mattress.

1 Cut three ruffle pieces using this formula: Ruffle top = mattress width + $1/2$" by length + $1/2$" (cut one); Ruffle skirt = length is distance to floor + $1 1/2$" and width is mattress length x 2 (cut two). (You may double and a half the fabric when cutting to create even more gathers, but this makes gathering more awkward.)

2 Hem two short sides and one long side of skirt.

3 Baste and gather unhemmed side of each skirt to measure length of mattress.

4 With right sides facing, sew each skirt ruffle to ruffle top long sides with $1/4$" seam allowance.

5 Narrowly hem short sides of ruffle top.

If bed or crib does not have floor-length head and end boards, sew additional ruffle skirts to ruffle top short sides.

❖ fitted ❖ sheet ❖

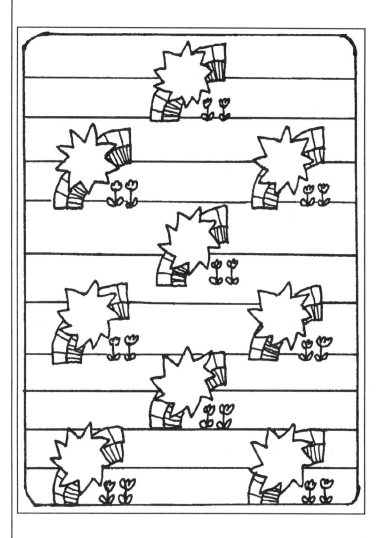

MATERIALS

cotton or flannel (1³/₄ yds.)

¹/₈" elastic (1 yd.)

scissors

ruler

thread

*A full-size crib mattress'
average measurements are
27" x 52" x 5" deep.*

❖

Cut squares on corners.

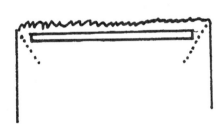

Sew elastic to gathered edges.

1 Measure mattress, and add 8" to all sides for fabric cutting size. Cut fabric.

2 Cut an 8" square from each corner.

3 With right sides facing, sew each pair of cut edges together with 1/4" seam allowance to form tucks.

4 Hem side edges.

5 Baste and gather top and bottom edges to reduce by 1/3. Cut elastic same size as gathered edges, and sew to gathered fabric.

❀ ❀ ❀ ❀ ❀ ❀ ❀

A nice gift is two fitted sheets and matching crib bumpers as described elsewhere in this book.

❀

· child's · coverlet ·

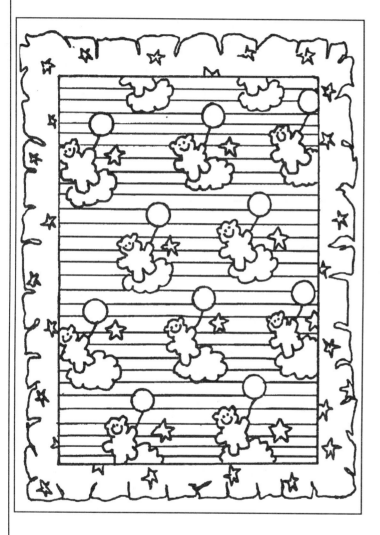

MATERIALS

pre-quilted fabric – 42" width (1yd.)

medium-weight cotton backing (1 yd.)

pre-gathered ruffle (4$\frac{1}{2}$ yds.)

straight pins

scissors

thread

iron

*This is a standard size cover.
Fabric stores frequently stock
pre-quilted panels with nursery motifs
for infant coverlets.*

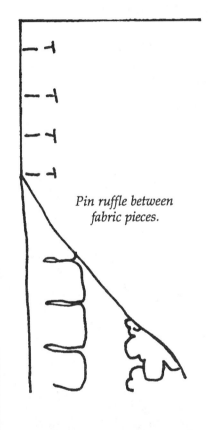

Pin ruffle between fabric pieces.

1 Cut 36" x 42" backing.

2 With right sides facing, pin both fabric pieces and ruffle together, with ruffle facing inward between pieces.

3 Sew all three pieces together on all sides with sufficient seam allowance to catch ruffle hem, leaving a 6" opening to turn out.

4 Turn out. Press.

5 Slipstitch opening closed.

Sew ribbon on completed coverlet for accent border. Embroider child's name, birthdate, or year given in coverlet corner.

crib · garland

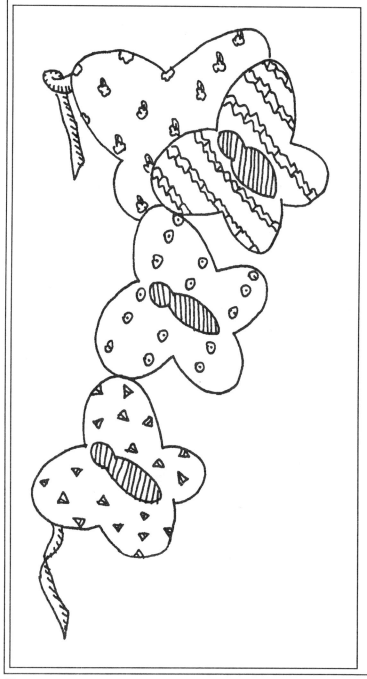

MATERIALS

various patterned cotton – 11" squares (5)

felt

scissors

thread

polyester stuffing

glue

1" ribbon (2/3 yd.)

Butterfly pattern is actual size. Tie garland ties securely to crib, and do not use fabrics that could endanger a child if placed in mouth.

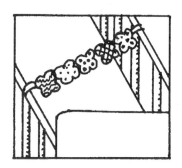

1 Cut one pattern on right side of fabric and one on wrong side for each butterfly.

2 Sew each butterfly together with right sides facing and a narrow seam, leaving a 1" opening. Turn out. Press.

3 Lightly stuff. Slipstitch opening.

4 Cut and glue felt body on one side.

5 Whipstitch butterflies' wingtips together. Cut ribbon in two, and sew one to each end wingtip.

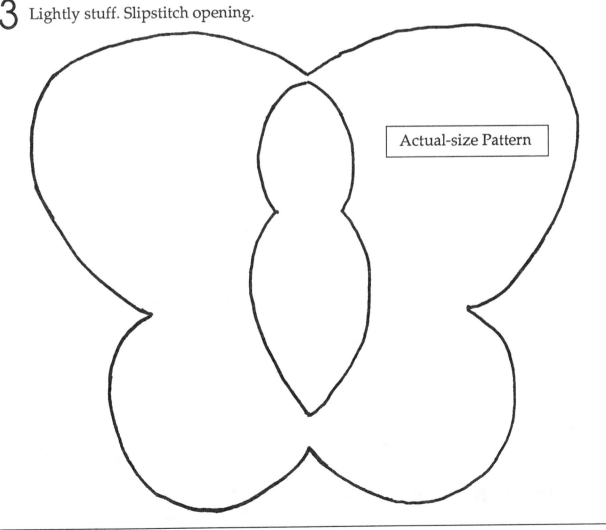

Actual-size Pattern

receiving ❁ blanket

MATERIALS

flannel (1¾ yds.)

scissors

thread

iron

❁

INSTRUCTIONS

1 Cut two 31" x 41" pieces.

2 Press edges ½" to wrong side of fabric.

3 With wrong sides of fabric facing, topstitch pieces together along all edges. Press.

Press edges to fabric wrong side.

A receiving blanket has many uses, such as a light bed cover, liner, or outdoor wrap. Make a blanket using complimentary colored or patterned flannel for backing. Or use cotton with a flannel backing for a second blanket.

❀ crib ❀ mirror ❀

Reflective plastic, commonly known by the brand name Mylar, is sold by plastic or glass companies in 2' x 3' adhesive-backed pieces. Infants will enjoy seeing their reflections in the mirror.

MATERIALS

cardboard (6" x 6")

reflective plastic (6" x 6")

pre-quilted fabric (7" x 7")

pre-gathered ruffle (20")

glue

1/2" ribbon (2/3 yd.)

❀

INSTRUCTIONS

1 Attach plastic to cardboard front.

2 Glue fabric to back.

3 Fold excess fabric to front, trim fabric bulk in corners, and glue fabric edges to front.

4 Glue ruffle to cover front fabric edges.

5 Make two holes in top corners for ribbon crib ties. Attach ribbons.

❖ infant ❖ nap ❖ roll ❖

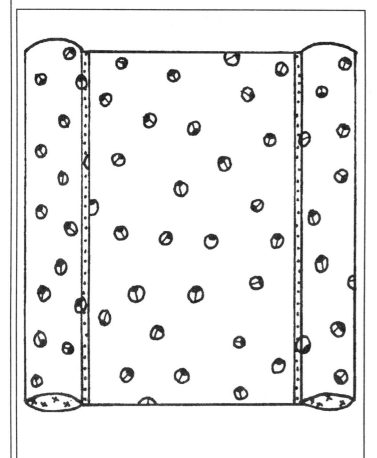

MATERIALS

medium-weight fabric (1½ yds.)

bolster fabric (¾ yds.)

ruler

scissors

iron

thread

polyester stuffing

Use nap roll as a portable sleeping area for infants too young to roll over or crawl. It's also handy as a diaper changing station.

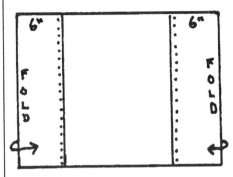

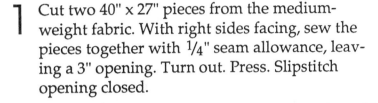

1 Cut two 40" x 27" pieces from the medium-weight fabric. With right sides facing, sew the pieces together with $1/4$" seam allowance, leaving a 3" opening. Turn out. Press. Slipstitch opening closed.

Fold sides in and sew down.

2 Fold 40"-side edges in 6" toward middle. Press fold line. Press side edge $3/4$" under, and top stitch edges to pad.

3 Cut two $12 1/2$" x 27" bolsters and four 6"-diameter circles. With right sides facing, sew long edges of one bolster piece together with $1/4$" seam allowance. Turn out. Repeat steps for other bolster.

4 With circle edges turned inward $1/4$", whipstitch one circle to bolster end. Turn and stuff. Whipstitch remaining circle on other bolster end. Repeat steps for second bolster.

Sew circles to bolster ends.

5 Slip bolsters into top or bottom of side openings.

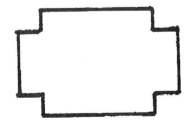

*Sew additional bolsters
to top and bottom for a more contained area.
Cut fabric as illustrated.*

* dream * pillow *

MATERIALS

cheesecloth or thin gauze (1/8 yd.)

potpourri mixture (3/4 oz.)

light-weight cotton (1/4 yd.)

batting – 36" width (1/3 yd.)

ruler

scissors

thread

iron

✿ ✿ ✿ ✿ ✿ ✿ ✿ ✿

Replace potpourri mixture after six months to keep pillow smelling sweet!

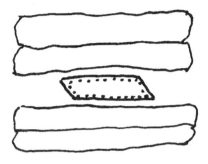

Put potpourri pouch between batting.

Put pillow in case and sew opening closed.

1 Cut two 5$\frac{1}{2}$" x 4" cheesecloth pouch pieces. Sew three sides together with a small seam allowance. Turn out.

2 Put potpourri mixture in pouch. Whipstitch open side.

3 Cut four 8$\frac{1}{4}$" x 11$\frac{1}{4}$" batting pieces. Stack batting, centering pouch between the second and third pieces.

4 Cut two 9" x 12" pillow case pieces. With right sides facing, sew case pieces together on three sides with a $\frac{1}{4}$" seam allowance. Turn out. Press.

5 Insert batting stack into case. Slipstitch open side closed.

Use hops, whose smell is associated with sleep inducement, instead of potpourri mixture.

❋ baby's ❋ tapes ❋

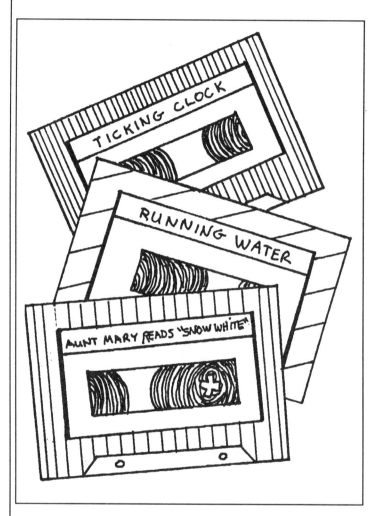

MATERIALS

cassette tape (60-minutes)

❋

INSTRUCTIONS

Using a 60-minute cassette tape, record rhythmic sounds, such as running water, electric fan, ticking clock, or piano metronome. This helps calm tired babies and is an excellent shower gift. For older children, record a story book on tape, and give them the book and tape. Read slowly, and say "Turn page" when you turn the page. Story tapes let you be with your little ones even when you have to be away. You might be gone for awhile, but you're still there to read them a bedtime story!

❋ ❋ ❋ ❋ ❋ ❋ ❋

• 5 •

Baby Basics

❖ carry-all ❖ tote ❖

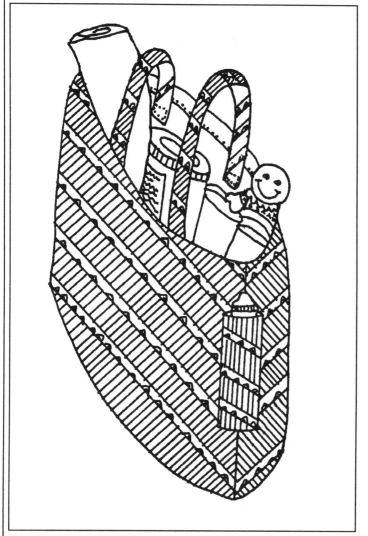

MATERIALS

sailcloth or outdoor canvas (3/4 yd.)

scissors

ruler

thread

iron

❖ ❖ ❖ ❖ ❖ ❖ ❖

Keep a plastic bag inside Tote for soiled diapers!

I · N · S · T · R · U · C · T · I · O · N · S

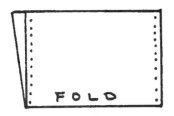

Seam side edges.

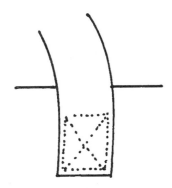

Sew strap ends to inside.

1 Cut one 28" x 17" bag piece, one 5" x 8" bottle pocket, and four 2" x 25" straps.

2 With right sides facing, fold piece to measure 14" x 17". Sew sides together with $1/4$" seam. Turn out. Hem top edge. Press.

3 Press bottle pocket edges under $1/2$". Center and topstitch bottle pocket's sides and bottom to a side seam 2" down from tote top. Hem pocket top edge.

4 Press edges of all strap long sides inward $1/4$". With wrong sides facing, topstitch each pair of straps together.

5 Sew 2" of strap ends to each side of inner bag.

*Add a front 10" x 13" pocket to tote by pressing
pocket edges under $1/2$"
and topstitching pocket to tote front.
You can also line the tote with water-resistant
fabric by basting a 28" x 17" lining to the wrong
side of sailcloth or canvas before
constructing the tote.*

child's • step-stool

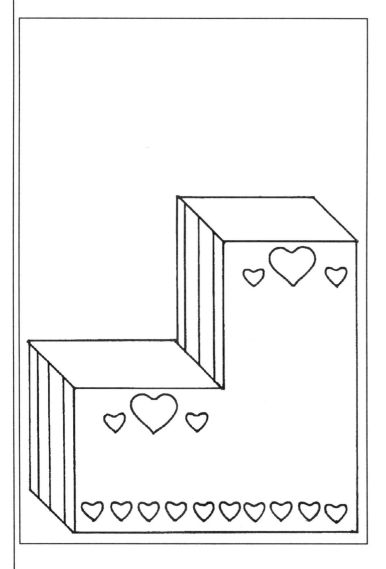

MATERIALS

$1/2$" interior plywood (2' x 4')

ruler

saw

wood glue

#4 $1^1/4$" finishing nails (about 22)

sandpaper

paint

Children can use these steps for hard-to-reach areas, such as sinks and counters, and assume responsibility for tooth-brushing and other grooming tasks.

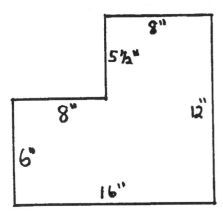

Side measurements.

1 Cut one 13" x 9" upper step, one 13" x 8" lower step, one 13" x 5½" upper step facing, one 13" x 12" back, and two sides using diagram.

2 Glue and nail back to sides, upper and lower step pieces to sides, and upper step facing to sides.

3 Sand, paint, and seal.

❖ ❖ ❖ ❖ ❖ ❖ ❖

Tack carpet scraps to step tops for extra slip-protection. Paint or stencil designs or child's name on step sides.

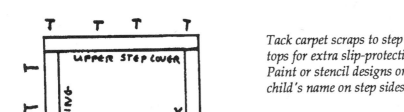

Nail step pieces together.

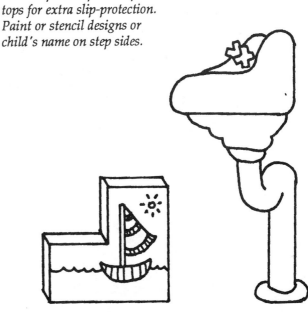

❖ seat ❖ cover ❖

MATERIALS

pre-quilted fabric (2/3 yd.)

pre-gathered ruffle (1 1/2 yds.)

ruler

scissors

thread

iron

*Use this cover
for highchairs, infant seats,
and some infant
car seats.*

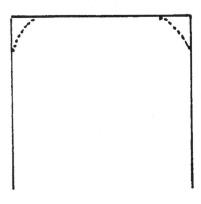

Round off top edges by cutting and seaming.

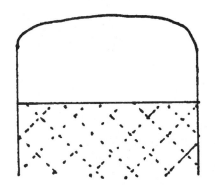

Sew flap to cover.

1 Make a paper pattern off the chair to be used, or cut two 16" x 24" pieces and one 16" x 6" flap for a standard-sized cover.

2 With right sides facing and lace pointing inward between the pieces, sew the two large pieces together with a 1/4" seam allowance, leaving the 16" bottom edges open. Slightly round off top edges while sewing for a better fit, as in diagram.

3 Turn out. Press. Hem bottom opening.

4 With right sides facing, sew flap top and sides to cover with 1/4" seam allowance.

5 Turn out. Press. Hem bottom opening.

If using for car and infant seats, cut slit for strap openings. Sew slit edges with closely-spaced blanket stitches.

watermelon • bib

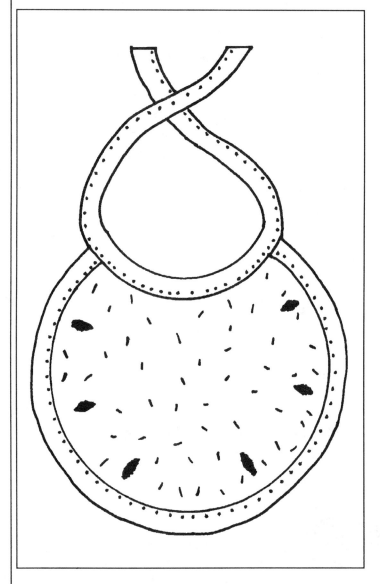

MATERIALS

hot pink terry cloth ($1/4$ yd.)

black embroidery floss

$1/2$" green double-fold bias tape (1 $1/2$ yd.)

scissors

straight pins

thread

iron

*You can use colorful washcloths,
which come in different sizes, to make
this and other bibs.
Thicker washcloths are best for
greater absorbency.*

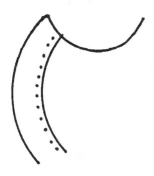

Sew tape to bib edges.

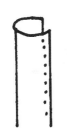

Stitch tape together for ties.

1 Cut out two 8"-diameter circles. Cut semicircle for neck opening. For infants, the semicircle will have a 2" diameter, and for older toddlers the diameter will be 3" to 4".

2 Embroider six black seeds with satin stitch on one bib circle. Mark seed position to help space seeds evenly. Begin sewing seeds 1" from circle sides.

3 With circles together, insert bib edges in bias tape fold. Tape fold should be flush with outer bib edges. Pin tape to edges. Sew tape to bib, except for neck opening.

4 Sew bias tape to neck opening, leaving 15" on each side for ties.

5 Topstitch tie sides together. Hem tie ends. Press bib and ties.

❖ ❖ ❖ ❖ ❖ ❖

Several handmade bibs adorned with embroidery, appliques, a name, or personalized touches you create make wonderful baby or shower gifts. Make several in different sizes, too!

❖ diaper ❖ holder ❖

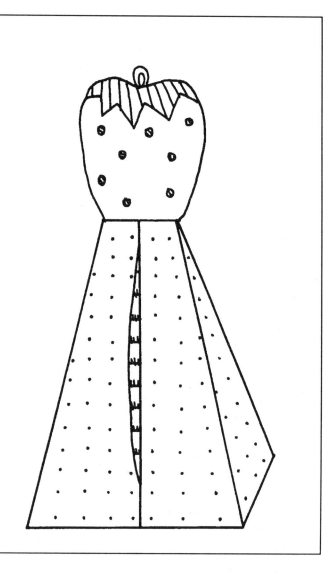

MATERIALS

red dotted-swiss cotton (1 $1/2$ yds.)

ruler

scissors

thread

iron

cardboard (9 $1/2$" x 13 $1/2$")

pink cotton or felt (22" x 20")

polyester stuffing

felt (black and green)

glue

❖   ❖   ❖   ❖   ❖   ❖

*Substitute a heart or animal head
for holder top. Design bottom will
overlap holder on both sides.*

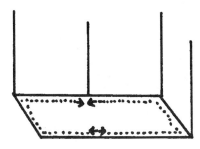

Begin sewing bottom at large midway dot.

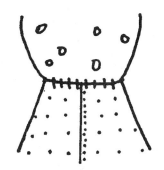

Hand-sew top folded under top edges to holder.

1 Cut from the dotted swiss two 25" x 27" holder pieces and one 10" x 14" bottom. With right sides facing, sew two 27" sides together with $1/4$" seam allowance, and narrowly hem the other two 27" sides.

2 With right sides facing, sew bottom to holder with $1/4$" seam allowance. Start sewing bottom at holder center seam and bottom midway point. Return to center seam to sew other half of bottom. Front edges will overlap. Press. Put cardboard on inner bottom for stability and shape retention.

3 Baste and gather holder top edges to measure 10" around.

4 Cut two strawberry pieces (10" x 11") from pink fabric and, with right sides facing, sew together with $1/4$" seam allowance, leaving the bottom 10" open. Turn out.

5 Slightly stuff strawberry, and whipstitch to holder. Glue green felt stem top and black $1/4$" diameter seeds to berry.

Fold a $1/2$" ribbon (1 $1/2$" long) in half and sew to top middle for hanging this clean diaper storage device on a nail in a wall. Or sew the ends of a folded 9"-long ribbon on holder top to hang off a door knob.

❖ changing ❖ pad ❖

Flannel-backed vinyl is the fabric used for table cloth covers. You might want to make several of these pads. Carry one in a diaper tote for away-from-the-house diaper changes, keep one at each of the diaper-changing stations in the house, or even place under bed sheets in case of accidents.

❖

MATERIALS

flannel-backed vinyl (1 yd.)

ruler

scissors

thread

❖

INSTRUCTIONS

1 Cut two 35" x 19" pad pieces.

2 Turn all edges under ¼", and topstitch pieces together close to the edges with wrong sides of vinyl facing.

3 Make a terry cloth cover, if you want, by cutting two 36" x 20" terry pieces. Sew terry pieces together as you did with vinyl, except leave one 35" side open for pad insertion. Hem edges of opening. Make two or more terry covers.

❖ wash ❖ mitten ❖

MATERIALS

colorful terry washcloths (2)

scissors

embroidery floss

thread

iron

❖

INSTRUCTIONS

1 Cut a paper template for pattern. Use pattern to cut animal face shape from each washcloth.

2 Embroider facial details on one washcloth.

3 With right sides of washcloths facing, sew top and side edges together with 1/4" seam allowance. Turn out. Press. Hem bottom edges.

Thick terry washcloths work well for older children, while the thinner washcloths are better for bathing infants, allowing you to gently wash in neck and leg folds.

❖ ❖ ❖ ❖ ❖ ❖ ❖

❖ shoulder ❖ pad ❖

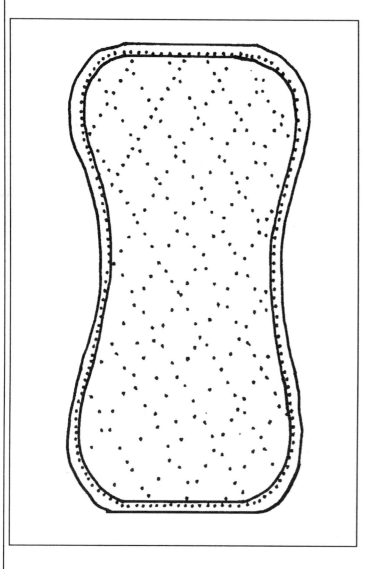

MATERIALS

paper ($16^{1}/_{2}$" x $8^{1}/_{2}$")

scissors

ruler

pre-quilted fabric ($^{1}/_{4}$ yd.)

$^{1}/_{2}$" double-fold bias tape ($1^{1}/_{2}$ yds.)

thread

*Pad is worn over shoulder
for spit-up protection while
burping baby.*

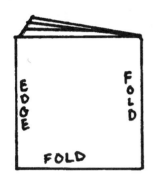

Fold paper into quarters.

1 Fold paper in half length-wise.

2 Fold again width-wise.

3 Cut pad pattern using diagram.

4 Unfold paper and cut two fabric pieces using pattern.

5 With wrong sides facing, join the two pad pieces and insert edges into fold of bias tape. Pin. Sew tape to pad around all edges.

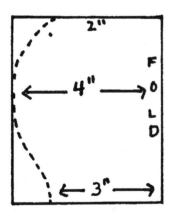

Cut paper pattern.

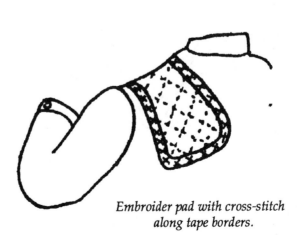

Embroider pad with cross-stitch along tape borders.

❖ hooded ❖ towel ❖

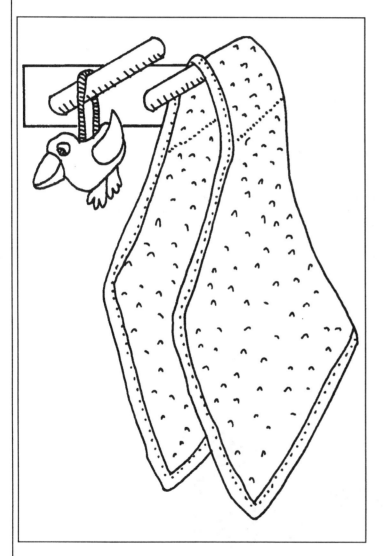

MATERIALS

thick terry cloth or terry velour (1 yd.)

ruler

scissors

thread

iron

This fits newborn to nine-month-old infants. Terry velour with its thickness and softness makes a sumptuous hooded towel for a freshly bathed infant.

I ❖ N ❖ S ❖ T ❖ R ❖ U ❖ C ❖ T ❖ I ❖ O ❖ N ❖ S

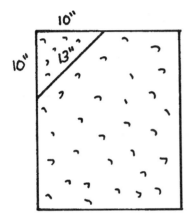

Sew hood to towel corner.

1 Cut a 34" x 30" towel and 10" x 10" x 13" hood triangle.

2 Narrowly hem hood on 13" side.

3 With right sides facing, sew both 10" sides to towel corner with a $1/4$" seam allowance.

4 Turn out. Press.

5 Use zig-zag stitch on all sides to prevent ravelling, or sew $1/4$" double-fold bias tape on sides.

The hood can be made from contrasting or complimentary toweling and trimmed along edges with embroidered ribbon.

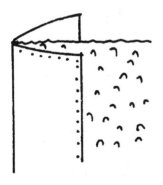

Sew bias tape on towel edges.

❖ stroller ❖ bag ❖

MATERIALS

pre-quilted fabric (1/2 yd.)

cotton lining (1/2 yd.)

ruler

scissors

thread

iron

2" wide Velcro strip (4")

Attach bag to stroller or carriage handles with Velcro straps to carry small items while out and about.

❖

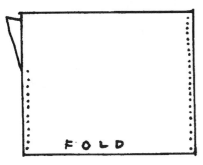

Seam sides together.

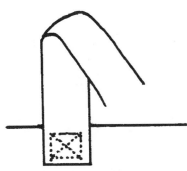

Sew strap end to inner purse.

1 Cut one 17" square from both fabrics. With right sides facing, sew squares together with $1/4$" seam allowance, leaving an opening. Turn out. Press.

2 Fold piece in half with lining on outside, and sew corresponding sides together with $1/4$" seam. Turn out. Press.

3 Cut four $2\,1/2$" x 8" straps. Press long sides inward $1/4$". Topstitch two straps together.

4 Sew one side of 2"-square Velcro tab to strap end. Sew adjoining part of tab to bag inside where strap will join ($1\,1/2$" down from bag top; 3" in from seams). Sew strap end without Velcro on opposite bag side ($1\,1/2$" inside of bag).

5 Repeat steps for second strap. Second strap will be attached to bag 3" in from opposite seam.

❖ ❖ ❖ ❖ ❖ ❖ ❖

Attach shorter straps at sides instead of front and back for umbrella stroller bags.

highchair ✦ mat

MATERIALS

artist's stretch canvas – 72" width (1$\frac{1}{6}$ yds.)

white latex paint

ruler

scissors

glue

paint (for design)

polyurethane sealant

Use vinyl with cotton backing for unadorned mat. Do not hem or seal vinyl mat.

Hem edges with glue.

Paint primer coat with latex.

1 Cut 45" mat square.

2 Cut 1" slits in each corner, and hem mat by gluing 1" of canvas to wrong side.

3 Paint both sides of mat with latex.

4 Pencil design on mat. Paint or stencil design.

5 Use three coats of sealant on topside of painted mat.

❖ ❖ ❖ ❖ ❖ ❖ ❖

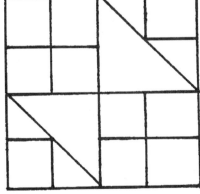

Use quilt block designs for mat decoration.

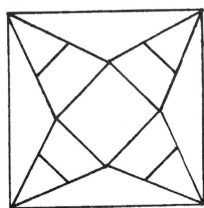

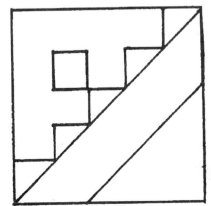

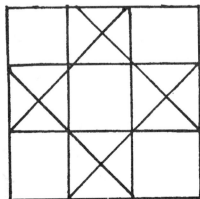

❖ infant's ❖ head ❖ support ❖

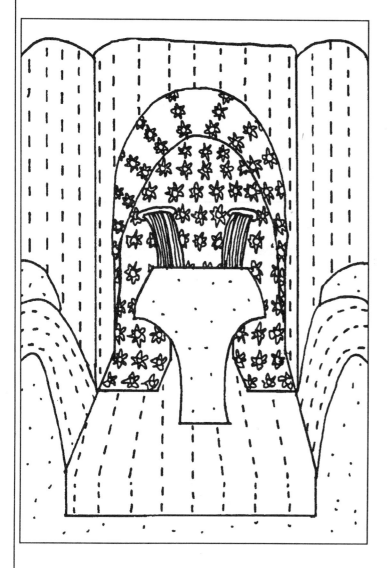

MATERIALS

cotton (1 yd.)

scissors

batting – 48" width ($1/3$ yd.)

polyester stuffing

ruler

straight pins

iron

thread

Velcro tabs – $3/4$" x $3/4$" (6)

Use this support in car seats, mechanical swings, and umbrella strollers for a head support when an infant is unable to hold head up.

I·N·S·T·R·U·C·T·I·O·N·S

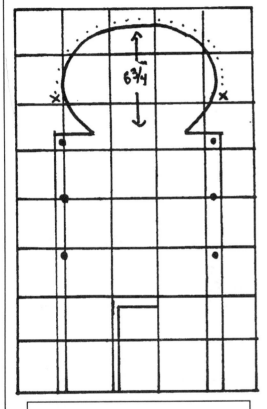

one square = 2"

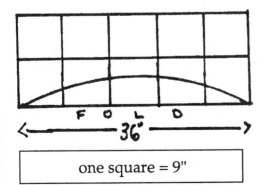

one square = 9"

1 Cut from cotton two support body pieces, one support upper border, and one double-layer of batting, as shown on diagrams.

2 With right sides facing and batting on one wrong side, pin and stitch support body pieces together with ¼" seam allowance, leaving 5" to turn out. Turn out. Press.

3 With right sides facing, fold border in half length-wise, and sew rounded top edges together with ¼" seam allowance, leaving 3" at one end unsewn. Turn out. Stuff.

4 With right sides facing and border centered on top of body piece, sew border to body piece along head section. (The head section is between the two x's as marked on the diagram.) Border ends attach with Velcro to the body piece.

5 Sew half of each Velcro tab to corresponding points on head border and body using circles on diagram for placement position.

For extra holding power, use snaps instead of Velcro tabs.

❖ galley · kit · ❖

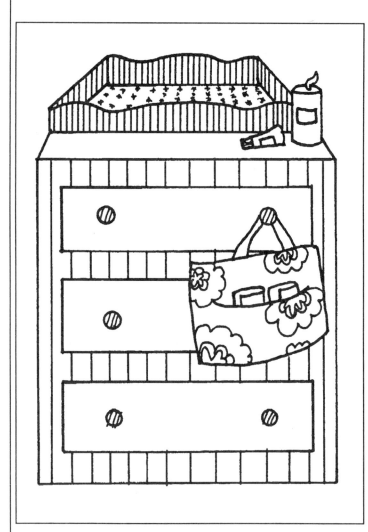

MATERIALS

1" x 6" pine, oak, or other board (9')

saw

wood glue

#6 1$\frac{1}{2}$" flathead woodscrews (8)

$\frac{1}{2}$" plywood (34$\frac{1}{2}$" x 11$\frac{1}{2}$")

#4 1$\frac{1}{4}$" finishing nails (12)

sandpaper

paint or wood stain

polyurethane sealant

❖ ❖ ❖ ❖ ❖ ❖ ❖

Galley kits are used on bureaus for diaper changing with a towel, folded blanket, or covered foam for an interior pad. Or use kit on bureau or table as an enclosed container for baby supplies.

❖

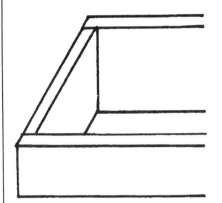

Front and back overlap side ends.

1 Cut two 6" x 3' pieces for front and back and two 6" x 11½" sides.

2 Cut curves on top edges or bevel edges, if desired.

3 Glue side pieces to front and back, and nail. The front and back ends will overlap side ends.

4 Nail plywood to kit bottom.

5 Sand, stain or paint, and seal.

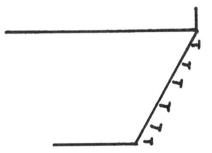

Nail bottom to kit through sides.

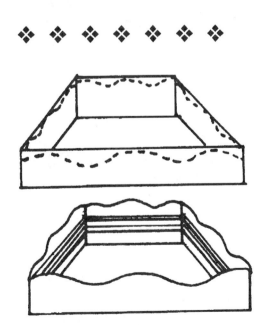

Use stencils and paint or dado blade on table saw to accent kit.

❖ gift ❖ basket ❖

Showers are generally given a month before or after birth. You may choose to decorate a plain basket yourself by painting it or weaving ribbons and dried baby's breath flowers through rim or handle.

MATERIALS

decorative basket

basket filler

infant items

ribbon

❖

INSTRUCTIONS

1 Line a basket with shredded wood filler, colored cellophane strips, or other filler.

2 Put inexpensive, individually wrapped presents in basket, such as: pacifier, baby magazine subscription, thank-you notes, bootie socks, diaper pins, training cup, parenting book, rattle, baby shampoo, sunblock lotion, or infant nail scissors.

3 Tie ribbon around basket top or handle.

• 6 •

Dressed For Fun

child's ⚘ backpack

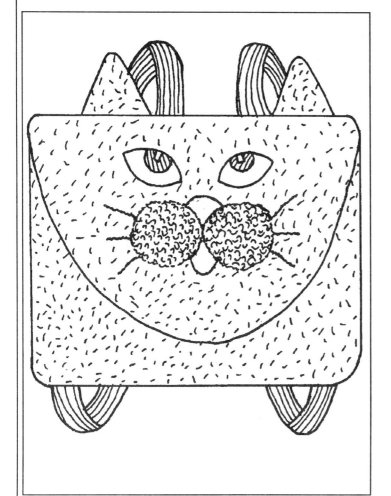

MATERIALS

fake fur (1/4 yd.)

ruler

scissors

thread

felt for eyes, nose, tongue, cheeks

pipecleaner for whiskers

polyester stuffing for ears

1" strap webbing (42")

1/2" Velcro (32")

Adjustable straps fasten on child's front!

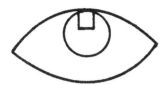

Green eye with yellow pupil.

Pink nose.

Pink tongue.

Pipecleaner whiskers.

1 Cut from fur one 9" x 6 1/2" front piece, one 9" x 2 1/2" bottom piece, two 2 1/2" x 6 1/2" side pieces, and one 9" x 12" back piece.

2 With fur sides facing, sew (with a 1/4" seam allowance) sides and bottom to front, bottom to sides, and back to bottom and sides. The upper part of the back piece will be the front flap.

3 Turn out. Cut rounded bottom edges on flap.

4 Cut facial details from felt. Whipstitch facial details, including 2" diameter felt or contrasting fur cheeks, the cut pipecleaner lengths, and the ears to flap face. (Illustrated eye, nose, and tongue are actual-sized.)

5 Cut four 10 1/2" webbing straps and four 8" Velcro strips. Sew straps to back. Top straps are 2" in from sides and 1" from top with Velcro strip on strap outside; lower straps are 1" in from sides and 1" from bottom with Velcro strip on strap outside. Velcro strips are sewn 2" down from strap attachment ends.

❧ ❧ ❧ ❧ ❧ ❧ ❧

Cut two 4" diamonds from fur used for pack for ears. Fold each diamond into a triangle, and lightly stuff with polyester stuffing. Whipstitch sides. Sew ears in front of straps.

appliqued sweatshirt

MATERIALS

18-month size plain sweatshirt

fake fur or fabric for face

cotton fabric for muzzle

polyester stuffing for muzzle

18 mm sew-on moving eyes (2)

fabric for bowtie and cap

thread

button for nose

embroidery floss for mouth

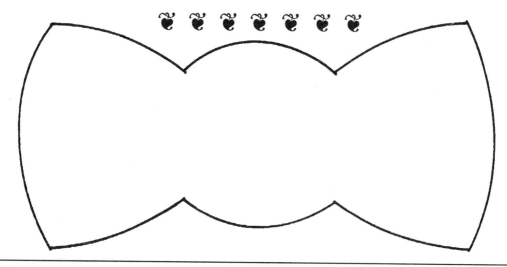

1 Copy pattern on appropriate fabrics.

2 Cut out pieces and topstitch or whipstitch to shirt.

3 Slightly stuff muzzle while sewing.

4 Sew eyes and button nose on very firmly, so child can not pull off.

5 Embroider mouth on muzzle.

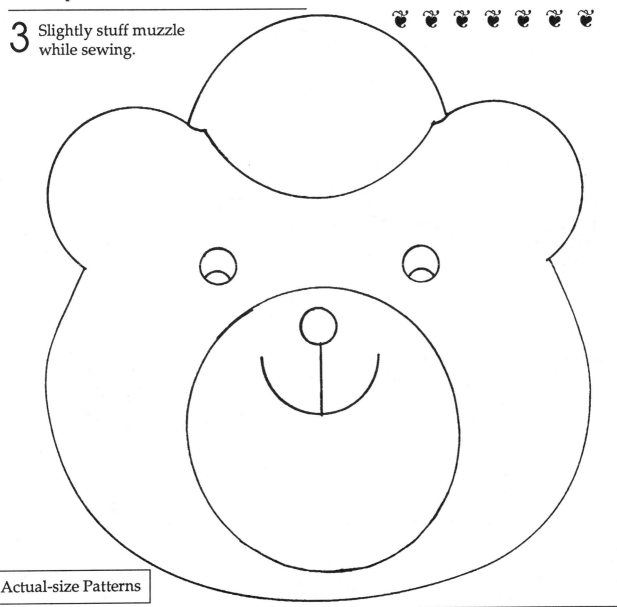

Actual-size Patterns

baby's cap

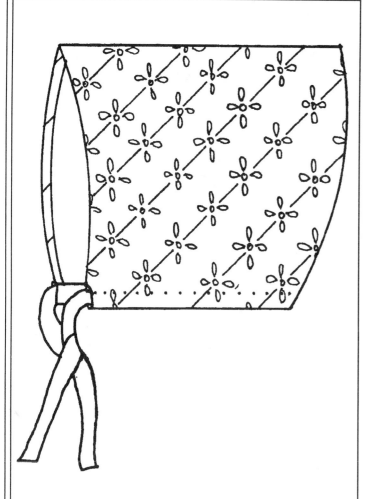

MATERIALS

light or medium-weight cotton (1/4 yd.)

ruler

scissors

thread

iron

safety pin

1/2" ribbon (1/4 yd.)

This cap is six-month size!

I · N · S · T · R · U · C · T · I · O · N · S

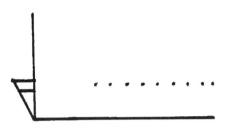

Sew casing at cap bottom.

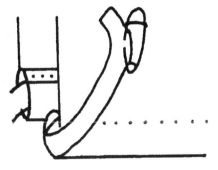

Use safety pin as ribbon guide.

1 Cut one 7$\frac{1}{2}$" x 15" cap piece from fabric.

2 Narrowly hem one long edge.

3 With right sides facing, fold to make a square. Sew the edges opposite hem together with $\frac{1}{4}$" seam allowance to enclose back of cap.

4 Make ribbon casing by sewing a $\frac{1}{4}$" hem around bottom of cap.

5 Thread ribbon through casing with safety pin on one ribbon end as a guide.

Use this cap with sewn-on ears for animal costumes. Slightly stuff ears to make them stand up.

bunting

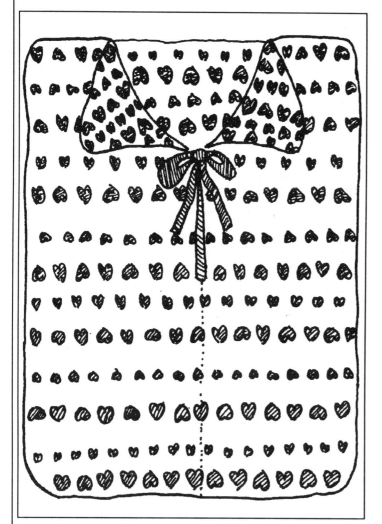

MATERIALS

pre-quilted fabric (1½ yds.)

ruler

scissors

1" ribbon (⅔ yd.)

straight pins

thread

iron

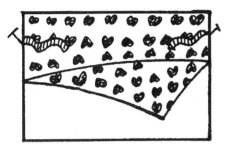

Pin ribbons to sides.

1 Cut two 26" x 38" bunting pieces from fabric and two 12" ribbon lengths.

2 With right sides facing, cut ribbon in half, and pin each ribbon 6" down from each corner of each 38" side. Sew pieces together with ribbons pointing inward on all sides with $1/2$" seam allowance, leaving 3" open.

3 Turn out. Press. Slipstitch opening closed.

4 Fold sides to middle. Bunting will measure $18^1/2$" x 25".

5 Sew center edges together with $1/4$" seam allowance from bottom to midway point (14"). Sew bottom of front and back together. Turn out.

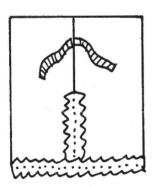

Seam front and bottom openings.

Line inside of back with flannel for extra warmth.

leg warmers

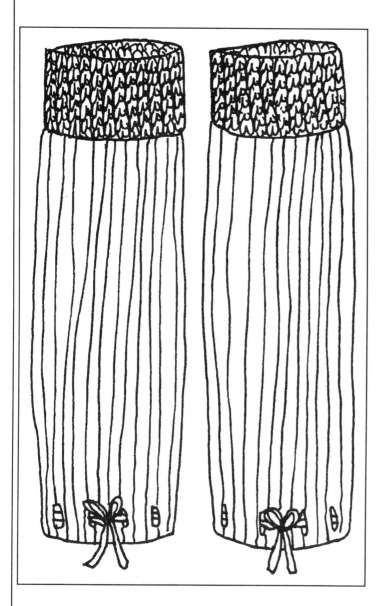

MATERIALS

infant or child-sized white sweater tights

6" white knit cuffs (2)

scissors

thread

white embroidery floss

$1/8$" satin ribbon ($3/4$ yd.)

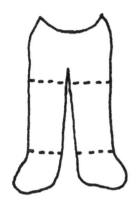

Cut warmers from tights.

Sew cuffs to warmers.

Sew white kneepads to inside of leg warmers for crawlers and fallers. To wear over overalls for extra warmth, use larger-sized tights to make warmers.

1 Cut foot and panty section from tights.

2 Fold each cuff in half so raw edges meet. With right sides facing, sew each folded cuff's raw edges to tops of each thigh opening. Turn out.

3 Turn ankle bottom openings under $3/8$" and sew to inside.

4 Make $1/4$" vertical slits $3/4$" apart on turned under ankle openings. Bind raw edges of slits with tightly-spaced blanket stitches using embroidery floss.

5 Thread ribbon in and out of slit openings, and tie bows with each ribbon to fit warmers to ankles.

Make duplicate stitches or embroider with contrasting yarn on stockinette sweater leg warmers to add color accents to warmers.

fun • t-shirts

Attach lace around collar.

Embroider alphabet on sleeves and seams.

Paint with textile paints.

Stitch a pre-made collar to neck opening.

Sew ribbons around collar.

Sew sequin applique.

Use an iron-on applique.

Sew material to shoulders.

Put rick-rack on seams.

Use rhinestone setter to attach rhinestones.

Batik with wax and dye.

Stencil a design.

bootie · socks

MATERIALS

bootie socks (1 pair)

contrasting embroidery floss

appliques – about 1" (2)

thread

INSTRUCTIONS

Make a knot with floss on each ball on cuffs; then two more knots on top of same knot. Sew applique above each toe seam.

Make a knot.

Cross-stitch across or sew small bow above toe seams.

hair ᘏ bows

MATERIALS

1/2" Velcro square or circle (2)

ribbons, small appliques, lace, or other decorations

thread

INSTRUCTIONS

Glue or sew decoration to one smooth side of fastener. These bows are for infants' and small children's hair that is too fine to hold ribbons or barrettes.

For older children, braid three thin ribbons on a barrette and let the ribbon ends stream down barrette sides. Or use a glue gun to attach closely-placed dried or silk flowers to a plastic headband to create a special occasion hair decoration.

Index to Projects

More Good Books from
WILLIAMSON PUBLISHING

PARENTS ARE TEACHERS, TOO
Enriching Your Child's First Six Years
by Claudia Jones

Be the best teacher your child ever has. Jones shares hundreds of ways to help any child learn in playful home situations. Lots on developing reading, writing, math skills. Plenty on creative and critical thinking, too. A book you'll love using!

192 pages, 6x9, illustrations.
Quality paperback, $9.95

GOLDE'S HOMEMADE COOKIES
by Golde Hoffman Soloway

"Cookies are her chosen realm and how sweet a world it is to visit."
Publishers Weekly

Over 100 treasured recipes that defy description. Suffice it to say that no one could walk away from Golde's cookies without asking for another...plus the recipe.

144 pages, 8¼ x7¼, illustrations.
Quality paperback, $7.95

THE BROWN BAG COOKBOOK:
Nutritious Portable Lunches for Kids and Grown-ups
by Sara Sloan

Here are more than 1,000 brown bag lunch ideas with 150 recipes for simple, quick, nutritious lunches that kids will love. Breakfast ideas, too!

192 pages 8¼ x7¼, illustrations.
Quality paperback, $8.95

PUBLIC SCHOOLS USA
A Comparative Guide to School Districts
by Charles Harrison

"How are the schools?" is the question most asked by families on the move whether it's cross-town, cross-state or cross-country. Finally, here's the answer as over 500 school districts in major metropolitan areas nationwide are rated on everything from special programs for high-or low-achievers to SAT scores, to music and art programs, to drop-out rates. If your children's education matters to you, here's a book you'll want to own.

400 pages, 8½ x11
Quality paperback, $14.95.

SIMPLY ELEGANT COUNTRY FOODS: Downhome goes Uptown
by Carol Lowe-Clay

An outrageously good cook brings country cooking to its pinnacle. A cookbook that's not fussy, not trendy — simply elegant. Everything from country fresh Pizza Rustica to Crumbed Chicken in Wine Sauce, Country Pork Supper, Sweet Cream Scones with Honey Butter to Whipped Cream Cake with Almond Custard Filling. Over 100 recipes capturing the freshness of the moment!

160 pages, 8x10, beautifully illustrated.
Quality paperback, $8.95

SUMMER IN A JAR: Making Pickles, Jams & More
by Andrea Chesman

"With recipes this simple and varied, it's hard to find an excuse not to preserve summer in one's cupboard."
Publishers Weekly

Chesman introduces single jar recipes so you can make pickles and relishes a single quart at a time. Plenty of low-sugar jams, marmalades, relishes. Pickles by the crock, too. Outstanding receipes.

160 pages, 8¼ x7¼, illustrations.
Quality paperback, $7.95

PARENTING THROUGH THE COLLEGE YEARS
From Application Through Graduation
by Norman Giddan, Ph.D., and Sally Vallongo

Don't drop out when your kids go off to college! They may need you in a different capacity, but they need you just the same. Here's all about this amazing 4 years in the life of parents and their almost-adult children. A lifesaver in many, many ways!

192 pages, 6x9
Quality paperback, $9.95

DINING ON DECK: Fine Food for Sailing & Boating
by Linda Vail

For Linda Vail a perfect day's sail includes fine food — quickly and easily prepared. She offers here 225 outstanding recipes (casual yet elegant food) with over 90 menus for everything from elegant weekends to hearty breakfasts and suppers for cool weather sailing. Her recipes are so good and so varied you'll use her cookbook year-round for sure!

160 pages, 8x10, illustrated.
Quality paperback, $9.95

AFTER COLLEGE
The Business of Getting Jobs
by Jack Falvey

Wise and wonderful...don't leave college without it. Filled with unorthodox suggestions (avoid campus recruiters at all costs!), hands-on tools (put your money in stationery, not in resumes), wise observations (Grad school? - why pay to learn what others are paid to learn better). You've already spent a fortune on textbooks. Now for only $10 you can have the most valuable book of all.

192 pages, 6x9
Quality paperback, $9.95

WHAT'S NEXT?
Career Strategies After 35
by Jack Falvey

Falvey explodes myths right and left and sets you on a straight course to a satisfying and successful mid-life career. Bring an open mind to his book and you'll be on your way. A liberating book to help us all get happily back into work.

192 pages, 6x9
Quality paperback, $9.95

TO ORDER:

At your bookstore or order directly from Williamson Publishing. We accept Visa or Mastercard (please include number, expiration date and signature), or send check to:

Williamson Publishing Company,
Church Hill Road, P.O. Box 185,
Charlotte, Vermont 05445.

(Phone orders: 802-425-2102.) Please add $1.50 for postage and handling. Satisfaction guaranteed or full refund without questions or quibbles.